Eli,
Thanks for your Encouragment
It's a joy working with you.
Jim Hanna
Ps 78:70-72

Leadership for L.I.F.E.

A Guide for Developing Leaders that Last

By
Dr. James G. Hanna

Table of Contents

Introduction

The coach's job was to get his players ready to face their crosstown rivals. He loved giving the team an inspiring pep talk before they left the locker room to begin their practice. This year's team was competitive but not dominant, as they lacked a big man who could outrebound their opponents.

The coach's pre-practice talk was especially passionate. At one point, he even lost his voice as he choked up with tears about the upcoming game. "Practice determines how you will perform," said the emotional coach. "If there is one team I want us to beat more than any other, it's this one." The speech caused quite an emotional stir in the locker room as the team leaders began yelling, getting the rest of the players excited. The team bolted out of the locker room, ready for an all-out effort.

As the coach and players made their way quickly to the court, they suddenly stopped in their tracks. Their frenzy was suspended. As the team stood there in silence, they realized their practice would either be delayed or canceled. What they discovered left them confused, frustrated and bewildered. What happened?

It appears that someone had broken into the gym during the night and removed the hoops. Without a goal to shoot for or a rim to aim, all the emotion and energy became useless. The hype was hoop-less.

Are We Developing Hoop-less Leaders?

As I think about the church and its capacity to develop high-impact leaders, I have wondered whether I have been guilty of developing hoop-less leaders. I think about the number of times I have asked someone to serve in a leadership capacity without helping that person understand what the goal was we were trying to achieve. There have been many times I have issued passionate pleas for volunteers without giving them a hoop to aim at or a goal to reach.

After talking with pastors and other church leaders about leadership training and development, I have often heard one of two responses. The first one is, I don't know where to begin. I would like to develop new leaders and strengthen our current ones, but I'm not sure where to start. A second response, if they are honest with me is, I would like to empower leaders, but I don't have the time. My schedule is too busy already..

Many pastors I know are doing all they can to prepare for the weekend services, keep the church budget in the black, deal with crises and conflicts within the congregation, and get more volunteers to help in the children's ministry. They have little time or energy to develop spiritual leaders. Any time they have to think about the future is usually spent focusing on the next series of messages or the next big event.

The result is that they often end up doing the majority of the ministry themselves. This practice can lead to a host of problems including health, emotional, and spiritual crises. They may either burn out or fall out of ministry altogether, neither of which is without damaging consequences. They are forced to come to grips with the reality that they have taken on more than God intended for them. There must be a better way–a way to develop leaders that is reproducible and transferable.

Developing Leaders Who Use Only One End of the Court

Many times in the search for leaders, we will find someone who is skilled in the business world and make that person a spiritual leader. If a person is financially successful or excels in business, we ask them to serve in the church.

Developing leaders who lack the moral character and spiritual maturity to handle the unique challenges of this leadership type can be detrimental in the long run. These leaders may make decisions based on self-gratifying principles rather than on God's Word and His agenda. Frequently, people who use only this end of the court make decisions based on what has made them successful. If there is an opportunity for self-advancement, they make the decision to move forward. If being in control gave them the advantage, they will lead God's people with this mindset. If they are a risk-taker, they may wonder why others with whom they serve are not on the same page. Often their bottom line decision is made on how much something costs, rather than on what God is leading His leaders to do about a situation. They lead by sight and not by faith. Consequently, when faced with pressure or pain from being a leader, they are apt to revert to responses that are less than Christ honoring. Using their natural instincts to deal with spiritual situations, they may go on the attack and strike back, or suddenly resign their leadership position. Neither of these are helpful to the organization, the leader, or the cause of Christ.

On the other end of the court, and usually more often the case, we take individuals of high character and ask them to be a spiritual leader. After they have prayed about it and talked to their spouse, they assume the position, but have no idea what skills are needed to lead.

The outcome is while being a tremendous moral support to others; they don't know how to lead. When asked to organize something, they aren't sure where to begin. If they need to motivate those under their leadership, they aren't sure how to communicate their ideas in a compelling and convincing manner. They are nice people, but are not capable of leading. They simply do not know how to take initiative, navigate through obstacles or resolve a conflict. They haven't learned how to use their leadership to empower others.

Developing Full Court Leaders

This book is about developing leaders who use both ends of the court. My desire is to see the development of leaders who serve efficiently, effectively and biblically.

Several years ago, I read a section of the Bible that changed the trajectory of my heart and mind. I came across a Psalm written by Asaph. This man was most likely David's worship leader who wrote several of the Psalms and originally put them to music.

As I read through Psalm 78, the words jumped off the page at me. I stopped, re-read them, and haven't stopped thinking about them since. Asaph pens these words to describe David being chosen as King over the people of God:

"He chose his servant, David, calling him from the sheep pens. He took David from tending the ewes and lambs and made him shepherd of Jacob's descendants-God's own people, Israel. He cared for them with a true heart and led them with skillful hands." Psalm 78:70-72

Like the coach who was very passionate about his team, I have used these words as a framework to develop leaders for over two decades. This passage is rich with principles that are needed to develop leaders who last. This book will use the acronym "L.I.F.E."

Those leaders who God uses most effectively are those who, first of all, are people who *lead a life of moral credibility*. Developing a Christ-like character is not the only thing that is needed for the spiritual leader, but it is the main thing. Asaph describes David as "caring for them with integrity of heart." David was also called "a man after God's own heart " (Acts 13: 22). These types of leaders are devoted to loving God and loving people. Without this devotion, they will not last as leaders. The first section of this book is focused on this topic. We will look at what it takes to lead a life of moral and relational credibility and how we can increase our integrity in a world filled with compromise.

Asaph also describes David as leading God's people with "skillful hands." Not only did he have a devoted heart, but he also had "skillful hands." The second key to being full court leaders is being able to *influence and inspire people with appropriate leadership skills*. In this section, we will look at several of the skills needed to lead God's people effectively. I have attempted to narrow it down to the most critical skills, and thought some may add to this list, I have found that these skills are essential in developing leaders for life.

A third area that Asaph refers to in describing David is his unique background and experiences. *"He chose his servant, David, calling him from the sheep pens. He took David from tending the ewes and lambs and made him the shepherd of Jacob's descendants- God's own people, Israel."* (Psalm 78:70-71)

Being a shepherd, David probably developed many of the skills he would need later to be "the shepherd of Jacob's descendants." God used David with his strengths and weaknesses, his phobias and faults, his mood swings, his compulsions, as well as his tender heart, and his love for God to shape him into one of the greatest leaders in the Bible.

The third quality needed to develop godly leaders is for them to *find their unique voice and lead from it*. These are leaders who lead from their strengths while being aware of their weaknesses.

As a spiritual leader, you too, have been given a unique personality. No one else like you has been called to lead. You may be an introvert or an extrovert. You may be a people person or a task-oriented leader. You have been given strengths, weaknesses, learned behavior as well as inherited characteristics. Using all of these traits, God has chosen to make you the person you are. In this section, we will look at the strengths you possess as well as the shadows of your leadership and how God can use your unique abilities and liabilities to impact others.

Finally, David was described as a person with a "true heart." This leads us to the final section of being a leader for life, *exercising heart-healthy habits*. It is your heart that fuels your character. In this section we will look at some of the spiritual practices you need to employ if you are going to move towards being a full court leader.

So there you have it, to develop leaders for LIFE requires:

L- Leading with moral credibility
I- Influencing and inspiring others with appropriate leadership skills
F-Finding your unique voice and leading from it
E- Exercising heart-healthy habits

How to Get the Most Out of This Book

• *Use it Personally*

This book is designed to be used individually or with a mentor, a small group or an accountability partner. Ideally, working through this book with someone enhances the learning process. This material was originally taught as a class, but it can also work well with two or three people in a mentoring group. Each chapter has discussion questions as well as additional resources for further exploration if you desire to go deeper on a certain topic.

- *Use it with Current Leaders*

You can use this with current leadership teams to strengthen and enhance them. After taking them through it, why not challenge them to invite a potential leader they know to go through this material?

- *Use it with Potential Leaders*

This book is designed with another in mind. You can take someone through this material one chapter a week for six months. Imagine what would happen if your emerging leaders were able to understand and begin practicing leadership principles that bring L.I.F.E.

Some launch points to keep in mind

- *Start Where People Are, Not Where You Want Them to Be*

When looking for someone to take through this material, whether it is one-on-one in a mentoring relationship, or as a group, it is important to realize that no one is qualified in all of these areas, including you.

What is most important is the direction of one's heart, not perfection. In order for the process of developing full court leaders to occur, you must be patient and grace-filled with those you lead. As a mentor of mine once said, "sheep will often act like sheep."

- *Focus on Progress, not Perfection*

There will be times when both you and those you are leading through this material will be tempted to quit. You will feel like you don't measure up. Guess what? You don't and that's okay. Most of the leaders in the Bible that God used didn't have it all together in order for God to use them. The key is making progress in your leadership, not perfection.

I encourage you to look at this material like train tracks. Sometimes you will need to slow down with those you are leading through this material. Other times, there are those who are extremely hungry to grow, and they can't get enough.

Sometimes you need to lean more heavily to the one side of the track called *relationship*. Like a train taking a curve, you focus on the relational aspect of the person you are leading. You may need to spend some time helping them through a conflict or crisis. On the other side, you lean more on the *curriculum* portion of the track, and focus more on the material of this book. Both are important, and one should not be neglected for the sake of the other.

There may also be times when you need to stop the train and let the person off. You have taken them as far as you can. Don't be tempted to bar the door and not let them off. Sometimes in order for new people to get on the train, some people need to get off of it.

• *Resist Your Reservations*

When considering utilizing materials like this, there are all kinds of reservations that arise. One such hesitancy is time. I don't have time. One thing you will read more than once in this book is this, you won't find time to do what's important; you have to make time. If you wait until you find the time, you won't find it. The truth is we make time for the things that are important to us.

The second form of reluctance is, I don't necessarily agree with everything written. You don't have to concur with everything an author writes to glean the principles that you can adapt to your setting. There may be some chapters in this book you skip; there may be others you want to add to, based on your life experiences. As my son-in-law says, "No worries!" You have my permission.

The reason we are attempting to develop leaders for L.I.F.E is because of the mandate that our Master, Jesus, gave us to "make disciples," as well as the Apostle Paul's instruction and example; *"You have heard me teach things that have been confirmed by many reliable witnesses. Now teach these truths to other trustworthy people who will be able to pass them on to others."* (2 Timothy 2:2)

• *This is a Pathway; it is Not the Only Path*

While I can attest to the fact that this material works in developing leaders, it is not the only path. When I take people through this material, whether it's teaching in a class, groups, or with individuals, I inevitably learn something new, something that I did not include. I would hope that this material is only the beginning of a life-long pursuit towards godly leadership. This book is titled "Leadership for L.I.F.E." It's my desire to develop learning leaders who will in turn teach others to use both ends of the court. My prayer is that the leaders in your sphere of influence will be those that bring life to others and follow one step closer to Christ, who is the ultimate example of leadership for life.

My challenge to you is to run the court, pass the ball, and see what happens. If God's in the game, you can't lose. He will build His church and His leaders, and the gates of hell cannot prevail against her. Who knows? In the process, you may find yourself developing leaders for L.I.F.E.

Talk it Over:

1. What are you hoping to gain by going through this material?
2. If you are going through this book with someone, share what your expectations are of your meetings together. How often will you meet? How long will you meet? (I would encourage you to meet weekly for six months for approximately an hour.) Where? Who will be part of this group?

When will you meet? _____

Who will you meet with? _____

Day/Time? _____

How long will you meet? _____

Dedication

This book is dedicated to all those who have
taken the "Leadership for L.I.F.E" course and encouraged
me to put this material into book form. Without your
positive response, this material would have remained
in a notebook on my shelf.

Acknowledgements

When it comes to writing a book of any kind it takes a team of people to make it happen. I want to first thank my amazing wife Elizabeth who encouraged me for years that I should put into writing the things I have been teaching.

I want to thank Donna Hoyt who took the earlier writings of each chapter and dissected them using her editor's knife. I also want to thank Lauren Heller who did an awesome job of formatting this manuscript into the appropriate style. I want to also thank those who served as initial readers of this material.

I want to thank Jack Mayer, Mark Humphreys, Terri Rhinehart, as well as Greg Carr and Doug Mello who encouraged me along the way to keep going.

I want to thank my Senior Pastor Dave Larson for his encouragement with this project and the incredible staff I serve alongside; Brett Avery, Kourtney Avila, Eli Arigotti, Leon Fox, Jon Nichols, Brian Benton, Janice Worsham, Jackie Lawrence, Tito and Jessica Valdespino, Michelle Perkins, Shaun Greenhalgh, Tatiana Sotelo, Sandi Amaral, Jack Mayer and many others.

Finally, I want to thank my Lord who rescued me and gave me the "why" for living. My prayer is that this material will help you take one step closer to Him and that you would know how much He loves you. He is the only one who can make you a leader for L.I.F.E.

About the Author

Jim Hanna serves as the Pastor of Spiritual Growth and Development at New Life Christian Center, a non-denominational church in Turlock, CA. Jim is responsible for caring for over 60 group leaders.

Jim has a passion to see a multi-layered approach to discipleship that includes groups, classes, mentoring and retreats.

Jim is a graduate of Moody Bible Institute, Diploma, Colorado Christian University, B.A., Trinity Evangelical Divinity School, M.Div., and Bethel University, D.Min.

Jim has been leading groups and leaders for over twenty-five years and has a desire to create as many environments as possible where people can take their next step closer to Jesus.

Jim has been married to his beautiful wife Elizabeth for 34 years and together they have three daughters and two sons, four grandchildren including twin grandsons. Jim loves football, basketball, bicycling, reading about leadership and playing racquetball.

Section 1

"Leading with Moral Credibility"

"He cared for them with a true heart."
Psalm 78:72

Chapter 1

"Is There a Leader in the House?"

*"If your actions inspire others to dream more, learn more,
do more and become more, you are a leader."*
John Adams

A pastor agreed to do the funeral service of a church member who had moved away. He traveled to a very small town where the former member had spent his last days. Upon arriving, the funeral director gave the clergy some brief instructions. He said, "At the conclusion of the service, you are to lead the procession of pallbearers out a side door." The director during this time went out to bring the hearse around to the side door.

The minister slowly walked in front of the casket and made his way to what he thought was the exit. Both he and his followers were greatly surprised! He mistakenly led the procession into a storage closet located next to the exit door. You can imagine the embarrassment as the entire group stopped and backed out of the closet.

I have wondered how many times leaders have led people into a storage closet rather than a doorway. We have not taken the time to gain an understanding of our context, to look around at our options, and have led our followers down a dead-end path. We can do that very easily if we don't know what we are looking for and what we are trying to accomplish. What is a leader? What makes a leader a spiritual one? How does this differ from natural leadership? In this chapter, we will define our terms. We will look at the various aspects of Christian leadership. Finally, we will look at the priorities of leaders that will set the pace for the remainder of this book.

The Leadership Diamond

A few years ago, I had the privilege of visiting the Smithsonian Institute and was able to stand in front of the Hope Diamond. Encased behind well-protected glass was one of the largest diamonds in the world. It was an amazing site to behold with its many facets. Its brilliance was breathtaking. People stood in hushed silence as they absorbed the beauty and enormity of this unique diamond. The subject of spiritual leadership has multiple facets as well. We will look at many of these in future chapters, but first let's glance at the entire diamond.

There have been a variety of definitions given by different leadership experts. Here are a few to consider:

"Leadership is a person who guides or directs a group."[1]
"Leadership is influence; it is not a position or a title."[2]
John Maxwell
"Leadership is the capacity and will to rally men and women to a common purpose and the character which inspires confidence."[3] Bernard Montgomery
"Leadership is moving people onto God's agenda."[4] Henry Blackaby
"Leadership is "a person influencing people to accomplish a purpose."[5] Pat MacMillian

Which of these definitions do you appreciate the most? If you are like me, you probably like portions of each. That's because each definition describes an element of spiritual leadership, but is not a comprehensive description.

Here is how I define leadership. Leadership is the capacity of one who *leads* with moral credibility, *influences* and *inspires* others with appropriate leadership skills, *finds* his or her leadership voice and *leads* from it, and *exercises* heart healthy habits, knowing that these habits are what fuel character and credibility. This is what I call "Leadership for L.I.F.E."

Consider God's choice of David:

> *"He chose his servant, David, calling him from the sheep pens. He took David from tending the ewes and lambs and made him shepherd of Jacob's descendants-God's own people, Israel. He cared for them with a true heart and led them with skillful hands."*
> (Psalm 78:70-72)

Look again at these verses and see if you can find the leadership for L.I.F.E. principles contained. God chose this unique individual named David, who knew how to shepherd sheep, and made him a shepherd over God's people. David cared for his followers with integrity of heart and with skillful hands.

What Makes Spiritual Leadership Unique?

It is important to understand that there is a difference between spiritual leadership and that found in other places. We sometimes want to take examples of guidance found in the marketplace and make them the standard by which to lead. While there are principles that we can incorporate from both the business world and sports world about leadership practices, it is important to realize that while related, they are not the same.

Moses was a great spiritual leader. In Exodus 33, he describes a significant distinction of spiritual leadership:

> "...*You have been telling me, 'Take these people up the Promised Land.' But you haven't told me whom you will send with me. You have told me, 'I know you by name, and I look favorably on you.' If it is true that you look favorably on me, let me know your ways so I may understand you more fully and continue to enjoy your favor. And remember that this nation is your very own people. The LORD replied, 'I will personally go with you, Moses, and I will give you rest- everything will be fine for you.' Then Moses said, 'If you don't personally go with us, don't make us leave this place. How will anyone know that you look favorably on me- on me and on your people- if you don't go with us? For your presence among us sets your people and me apart from all other people on earth.' "*
> (Exodus 33:12-16)

Did you catch it? Moses is saying that the one thing that sets spiritual leadership apart from all others is that biblical leadership makes sure that God is in the middle of all of its decisions. Moses was dependent upon God so much that he did not want to move unless God led him.

Moses gives us a second unique feature in the book of Numbers. He appealed to God saying, *"Please appoint a new man as leader for the community. Give them someone who will guide them wherever they go and will lead them into battle, so the community of the LORD will not be like sheep without a shepherd."* (Numbers 27:16-17)

Moses makes it clear that a spiritual leader, unlike a natural one, is appointed by God. While people may have a part in the process, it is ultimately God who selects the godly leader. Moses asked God for a person who would guide them and lead them into battle. Moses introduces us to the concept of spiritual leadership being a battle, a conflict against unseen adversaries. He reminds us that spiritual leaders must be aware of and deal with the spiritual resistance that will inevitably occur.

Finally, Moses asks God for a leader who has a shepherd's heart, someone who will lead and feed God's people. A spiritual leader does not use people as a means to his or her own end. Christ-like leaders authentically care for those people under their leadership. Sometimes that means loving someone enough to be honest with them, but even when doing so, making sure it is wrapped in love and concern for that person.

Eventually, the person that Moses is asking for here would be answered in the person of Joshua. When you read the book of Joshua, you can see how he exemplifies these qualities mentioned.

Moses describes the third mark of a spiritual leader; *"For what great nation has a god as near to them as the LORD our God is near to us whenever we call on him?"* (Deuteronomy 4:7) A spiritual leader is one who seeks God's agenda, His approval, His leading and His strength to move forward.

In the New Testament, Paul makes a clear distinction between spiritual and natural leadership. At the conclusion of 1 Corinthians chapter one, and the entirety of chapter two, Paul clarifies the contrast between human and God-like leadership. I encourage you to read these verses slowly and carefully in their context. At the conclusion of his discourse he writes, *"But people who aren't spiritual can't receive these truths from God's Spirit. It all sounds foolish to them and they can't understand it, for only those who are spiritual can understand what the Spirit means…But we understand these things, for we have the mind of Christ."*

Paul tells us that those who have placed their trust in Christ and His finished work on the cross have been given "the mind of Christ." This is why they can understand the leading and promptings of God's Spirit.

The Priorities of a Leader

Now that we have defined our terms and made a distinction between natural and spiritual leadership, let's take a few moments to focus on what the priorities are of a spiritual leader. Let's use the acronym L.E.A.D.E.R.S.

L- Learning

A leader must have a teachable heart. He or she must be willing to continue to learn more and more about how to sharpen his or her skills and gifts. In this day and age, you must learn to be selective in what you read. It's important to read and learn in the areas that will benefit you the most. Jesus said; *"Blessed are those who hunger and thirst for righteousness, for they will be filled."* (Matthew 5:6) One of my favorite Proverbs is; *"Instruct the wise and they will be wiser still; teach the righteous and they will add to their learning."* (Proverbs 9:9)

All effective leaders are learners. The moment you stop learning is the moment you stop growing as a leader. If physicians practice medicine and lawyers practice law, then it must also be true that spiritual leaders practice leadership.

As a leader, it is crucial to recognize the importance of your personal growth. You as a leader cannot lead people further than you have gone yourself. The greatest contribution you can make to people is learning to lead yourself well. C.S. Lewis said that "every person is composed of a few themes."[6] In this information age, you need to be selective in your learning. Let me suggest three topics on which to focus.

First, concentrate on the area of your *responsibility*. It is important to continue to sharpen your skills as a leader. One way to do that is to take advantage of the many webinars, e-books, podcasts, conferences, books and other means that relate to your area of leadership.

Secondly is the area of *personal development*, learning and reading in areas that you want to see God develop in your life. As a follower of Jesus Christ, His Spirit will reveal areas in which you need to grow and develop. When He does, write it down, and then ask God to guide you to resources that will help you grow in that area. It could be your marriage, parenting or some area of personal discipleship.

Finally, it's important to continue to learn *leadership development*. It's important to use the experiences of others as a form of mentorship in learning how to lead people. The fact that leadership is so much about relationships, I attempt to read frequently on this important topic. When I pastored and taught every week, I had a series at least once a year on relationships. If I could sum up the Christian life in one word it would be relationships; our relationship with Jesus Christ and with others.

E- Example

The leader is a pacesetter. He or she sets the tone and direction for the team. Someone has said, "Speed of the leader, speed of the team." A leader must be able to model how he or she wants others to follow.

The Apostle Paul wrote, *"Follow my example, as I follow the example of Christ."* (1 Corinthians 11:1) Earlier he wrote,

"Therefore I urge you to imitate me." (1 Corinthians 4:16) Paul was able to challenge others to live their lives the way he lived his.

When I grew up, I was told at times, "Do as I say, not as I do." That form of leadership does not lead followers to buy in to the leader's values and vision; rather, it promotes hypocrisy. As a spiritual leader, you cannot lead people to do something you are not willing to do yourself.

A- Available

Being available means that the leader is both available to God and others. Would you agree or disagree with this statement? God is more concerned about your availability than your abilities. If you make yourself available to God, He will use you even if you are not naturally gifted to do it.

God wants us to make ourselves available to Him and His mission in the world. *"Therefore, I urge you, brothers and sisters, in view of God's mercy, to offer your bodies as a living sacrifice, holy and pleasing to God- this is your true and proper worship."* (Romans 12:1)

Being available also means that the leader is approachable. People are not afraid of him or her. This means that the leader is not defensive all the time, particularly when he or she hears things that challenge his or her position. Being accessible does not mean that you never set boundaries and make yourself unavailable to people. Last time I checked there is only one Messiah who can be in all places at the same time, available to anyone in need, and you are not Him. What we are talking about is an attitude and demeanor that says you can be approached with anything.

Someone once told me it's important as a pastor and a leader to walk slowly through the auditorium and hallways both before and after the service. What they meant was that sometimes we can become so focused on our task that we forget that the public services are the only time of the week where such a large number of people will be gathered at the same time. It may be one of the few times that you will be able to connect with someone as a leader.

The pastor I serve under is great at this. During each of the weekend services, he stands out in front of the building and greets people as they enter. I'm sure that he has many things he could be doing, but I cannot tell you how much this has impacted people. He doesn't hide in his office or focus only on his own concerns. He rises above how he feels and makes himself available.

Now when our pastor is gone, you will find one of the staff following his example. Many people can't believe that the pastor who will be speaking that day is the one who greeted them as they came in. This has been one way we have reduced the perception that our church is a large impersonal church where no one even says "Hi," when they walk in.

D- Devoted

A leader must be a devoted person. He or she must be committed to God and people. A spiritual leader must make his or her relationship with Christ a top-drawer priority. He or she must take the time feeding and strengthening his or her soul in order to lead God's people.

Second, a spiritual leader must be committed to people. If you do not love people, you will not be a leader. You may be a boss, but you are not a leader. We must develop a caring heart.

Loving people has nothing to do with personality type. You may be an extrovert who loves people or an introvert like me, but the bottom line is you must be devoted to people. People will disappoint, frustrate, drain and challenge you, but at the end of the day, if you have not influenced others and shown Christ's compassion to those He gave His life for, you are not a leader.

E- Encouraging

The leader must be a coach, reassuring his people and motivating them. As one pastor has said, "leaders are dealers of hope." I know of a pastor who went from being a dope dealer before Christ to a hope dealer after Christ. In other words, a leader must impart hope and confidence to people he or she is leading.

A leader must get in the habit of giving verbal vitamins to people on a regular basis. This world has a way of taking its toll on people. This influence, along with the spiritual resistance that comes when you serve, can easily discourage followers. The writer of Hebrews says, *"But encourage one another daily, as long as it is called 'Today,' so that none of you may be hardened by sin's deceitfulness."* (Hebrews 3:13)

Here are three verbal vitamins to give others on a daily basis to help encourage them.

1. Praise them when they did a good job. Catch people doing good and point it out. Celebrate and encourage what you want to see happen. Tell their story, write a note or say it personally. People can't get enough praise for doing good things.

2. Encourage them to hang in there when times are tough. People need hope when they are going through tough times. They need reminding of the promises of God and the truth of what God's Word says about them and their situation.

3. Challenge them to do an even better job. We need to call out greatness in another. It's interesting that part of encouragement is admonishing. This means we are to challenge people to even greater faith and effectiveness. We have to be careful, however, to do so with a loving and grace-filled heart. Speaking of Christ, Paul writes; *"He (Jesus) is the one we*

proclaim, admonishing and teaching everyone with all wisdom, so that we may present everyone fully mature in Christ." (Colossians 1:28)

Question: Which is easier for you to give, positive encouragement or truthful admonishment? Which of these two do you need more of in your life right now? Why not ask God to give you what you need most in this area and see what happens?

R- Reliable

A spiritual leader must be a dependable person, one who keeps his or her word, one who keeps his or her commitments. Recently in a meeting we were asked to give a synonym or phrase for accountability. I thought of an accountant and mentioned the idea of being counted or counted upon. That's what it means to be a reliable leader.

Paul wrote to a younger leader in the church named Timothy, *"And the things you have heard me say in the presence of many witnesses entrust to reliable people who will also be qualified to teach others."* (2 Timothy 2:2)

Being reliable means I have to deny my feelings and do what I said I would do. If I can't, then I will either communicate that with my supervisor or I will find another reliable person who can replace me. David put it this way when describing someone who is a person of integrity; they *"keep their promises even when it hurts."* (Psalm 15:4) At this point it's okay to say Ouch!

S- Servant

A spiritual leader is one who humbles himself before the Lord and people. He or she realizes that the ministry is not a place to make a name for him or herself, but to make Jesus great by serving Him and serving others. A pastor I worked with once said that when he entered the ministry, he was given a towel by those who ordained him, symbolizing that the ministry is about being like Jesus and serving others.

Jesus taught about the difference between natural and spiritual leadership while here on Earth. In Mark 10: 42-45, Jesus said that the leaders of this world use their position and power to control and manipulate people. But Jesus told his disciples, his future leaders, this, *"among you it will be different. Whoever wants to be a leader among you must be your servant."* He concluded His teaching by disclosing His mission on Earth. *"For even the Son of Man came not to be served but to serve others and to give his life as a ransom for many."* (Mark 10:45)

Some have said we are never more like Jesus than when we are serving. You can serve without loving, but you cannot genuinely love others without serving.

The above qualities must become a priority for a person to be a dynamic, effective leader. Without them, we can easily find ourselves walking into storage closets instead of doorways.

I want to encourage you to look back on these priorities and choose one to meditate upon throughout the day. Then, each day take another and ask God to reveal to you how you can practice this during your day. There are seven of them, one for each day. There just may be a leader in the house, and it's you!

Talk it Over:

1. Which definition of leadership means the most to you?
2. Which facet of a leader's priorities do you agree with the most?
3. Who has been an example to you of an effective leader?

4. When did you first sense in your life that you had potential leadership qualities?

Going Deeper:

Blackaby, Henry T. and Richard Blackaby. *Spiritual Leadership: Moving People on to God's Agenda.* Nashville: Thomas Nelson, 2001.

Maxwell, John C. *Developing the Leader Within You.* Nashville: Thomas Nelson, 1993.

Sanders, J. Oswald, *Spiritual Leadership: Principles of Excellence for Every Believer.* Chicago: Moody Press, 1994.

Chapter 2

The Leadership Leverage

"Character is doing the right thing, not necessarily the easy or popular thing."
Source Unknown

J ames Kouzes and Barry Posner, in their book "Credibility," surveyed hundreds of business leaders and employees to determine the most desirable quality of a leader and those whom they work alongside. When asked what they prefer most in a leader, they were given twenty different character qualities and were instructed to rank them in order of importance. Of those surveyed, 87% said that honesty was the most important quality in a leader.

When asked the same question using the same qualities of what they desired most in a colleague, the response was almost the same. This time "honesty ranked number one at 82%." [1]

People still expect their leaders and co-workers to be people of integrity. Despite repeated attempts by our culture to emphasize that our private lives do not affect public action and in a world of increasingly blurred lines, people still expect their leaders to be people of principle and integrity.

Defining Integrity

Do you remember in elementary school that whole numbers were called integers and portions of whole numbers, fractions? Integrity means there is wholeness to our lives. This means that Christ is at the center of our lives as leaders and, therefore, He influences every area of our being. The dictionary defines integrity as "the state of completeness or wholeness, honesty, and sincerity." [2]

"Integrity is integrating my heart's values into my daily actions."[3] In other words, my actions and my words match up. What I say and what I do are congruent. The Bible describes someone who lives an inconsistent life as *"double-minded, unstable in all his ways."* (James 1:8 ESV)

It is important to understand that integrity does not mean perfection. No leader is one hundred percent consistent in all of his or her behavior. While perfection isn't needed to obtain integrity, humility and honesty are required. God says *"He gives grace to the humble,"* (James 4:7) *and* so do others.

I appreciate what Chuck Swindoll says about integrity, "I don't think we can take 'blameless' to mean simply 'without blame, without sin'; in that sense, I've never met anyone blameless. I'm certainly not. The point is that when we do fail, we say it. Integrity means we don't hide our stumble; we don't act like we didn't. Of course, there's some point on the spectrum of sin where disqualification for church leadership occurs. When you can sin and live with it, you're in trouble."[4]

Now that we have defined integrity, let's look first of all at things that can damage our credibility. These are things that can lead us to become double-minded.

Things that Injure our Integrity

1. *Selfishness-* selfishness is when life becomes all about me...my needs, wants, and desires. While most spiritual leaders would not acknowledge that we struggle with greed, the writers of Hebrews says, *"Don't love money; be satisfied with what you have. For God has*

said, 'I will never fail you. I will never abandon you.'" (Hebrews 13:5)

Have you felt God is distant from you, or maybe He has forgotten you? Could it be that your finances have come between you and God, so that when you look at God all you see is your financial situation? Jesus cautioned us against the subtle power of greed when he said, *"Be on your guard against all kinds of greed; life does not consist in an abundance of possessions."* (Luke 12:15 N.I.V.)

2. *Living in fear of people-* When we live in fear of what others think more than what God thinks, our integrity begins to decline. When we fear others' disapproval more than God's, we are heading down a slippery slope. Again the writer of Hebrews says, *"So we say with confidence, 'The LORD is my helper, so I will have no fear. What can mere people do to me?'"* (Hebrews 13:6)

Fear is the opposite of faith. Faith believes the best is going to happen; fear believes the worst will happen. When we worry about what others may say more than what God thinks, we injure our integrity. Here are some of the fears many spiritual leaders struggle with on an ongoing basis:

- Fear of rejection- being worried that we will offend others, and they will reject us.
- Fear of failure- not attempting great things for God due to past failures or what might happen if we try something.
- Fear of intimacy- many spiritual leaders have been wounded so deeply and frequently in ministry they refuse to open their heart up and get close to people.

- Fear of the future- what might happen to our ministry and us personally. We become driven by what others are thinking about our performance.

3. *When we lose touch with the God of integrity.* When we start leaning on our own understanding rather than seeking the mind of Christ, this leads to frustration and failure. Whether through busyness or neglect, we can miss spending time with the Lord and soon drift towards mediocrity and compromise in our life.
4. *When we associate with people who lack integrity-* Let's face it, who we choose to befriend has an influence on our attitude, actions, and integrity. The Apostle Paul put it this way, *"bad company corrupts good character."* (1 Corinthians 15:33- NLT)

When we choose to align ourselves with people who are negative, inclined to gossip, or are critical or angry, our character becomes contaminated. Andy Stanley says, "Your friends will determine the direction and quality of your life."

5. *When we practice destructive habits in our lives.* When we allow sin to remain in our hearts instead of repenting, our service to others and God suffers. It doesn't mean that we will never sin. However when we do, we must realize that we have grieved the Holy Spirit, confess our sin to God and return to Him.

Paul wrote these words, *"Don't be misled-you cannot mock the justice of God. You will always harvest what you plant. Those who live only to satisfy their own sinful nature will harvest decay and death from that sinful nature. But those who live to please the Spirit will harvest everlasting life from the Spirit."* (Galatians 6:7-8)

How Do I Increase My Integrity?

1. *Authenticity-* Integrity comes from letting people see the real me. Authenticity includes allowing people to see my struggles as well as my success. John Maxwell says, "Image is what people think you are; integrity is what you really are." [5]

2. *Accuracy-* Am I accurate with the statements I make? Is what I'm saying exaggerated or not? Is what I am saying based on hearsay or is it from the primary source?

3. *Consistency-* Do I do what I say I will do? Do I keep my word? Am I willing to do what I ask others to do? These are all questions about consistency. Integrity is not about perfection but rather about consistency. Fred Smith says, "effective leadership...is not based on being clever, it is based primarily on being consistent."[6]

4. *Possessing Personal Values-* Is my behavior guided by my beliefs? Do I have a set of priorities that are driving my life, or is there a sense of duplicity in my life? Do I act one way in public and another in private?

5. *Intimacy-* Integrity builds by allowing people to get close enough to me that they see my heart, my vision, what makes me laugh and what makes me cry. I can keep up my image from a distance and fool people, but I can only influence people up close.

6. *Being committed to the truth-* When we live our lives committed to pursuing and practicing the truth, integrity is built. When we have a passion for knowing what God says and practicing it, our credibility appreciates.

7. *By giving of yourself-* When you realize that you have been given your leadership gifts to serve others, and that it's not about people serving you, your relational credibility rises. Jesus said it this way; *"There is no greater love than to lay down one's life for one's friends."* John 15:13- NLT

8. *Humility-* When we are humble and admit that we don't have all the answers and that God is still at work in us, growing and maturing us, it gives people the ability to relate to us. It may seem counterintuitive, but people respect someone who is aware of his or her humanity and acknowledges it more so than one who does not.

9. *When you endure hardship-* The person who walks with God through the seasons of life and remains faithful creates moral credibility with those who know him or her. When you endure hardship and remain joyful and peaceful, when you resist being resentful, when you refuse to retaliate when evil is directed at you, your value as a leader expands.

10. *Time-* While time alone isn't all there is to integrity, it can be increased over a period of time as people see that you are a person who practices integrity.

Bronnie Ware was a nurse who worked with dying patients. She spent much of her time with dozens of people during the last three to twelve weeks of their lives.

While spending time with these terminally ill patients, she asked them questions and then recorded their responses. She asked, "Do you have any regrets? Or "Is there anything you would do differently?" There are five common themes she found, and she has written about them.

The most common response given was; "I wish I'd had the courage to live a life true to myself, not the life others expected of me."[7] What these patients were referring to is integrity, having the integrity to be true to yourself.

I want to challenge you to be who God created you to be. Don't be an imitation of someone else. Be the authentic person that God designed you to be and you will increase in integrity.

Talk it Over:

1. Who in your opinion is a person of integrity?

2. Which of the above qualities means the most to you?

3. Which of them will you ask God to help you develop in your life?

Going Deeper:

Dyer, Charles H. and Charles R. Swindoll. *Character Counts: The Power of Personal Integrity.* Wheaton: Crossway, 2010.

Kouzes, James M. and Barry Z. Posner. *Credibility: How Leaders Gain and Lose It, Why People Demand It.* San Francisco: Jossey-Boss, 2011.

MacArthur Jr., John F. *The Power of Integrity: Building a Life Without Compromise.* Wheaton: Crossway, 1997.

Chapter 3

Building your Trust Fund

"Trust is like a forest. It takes a long time to grow and can burn down with just a touch of carelessness."
David Horsager

"I just don't trust you anymore." I listened as a pastor shared with me what a couple told him during a final conversation they had with him before they left his church. He conveyed with a weak and wounded voice how devastating it was for him to hear that statement. "Why would someone say that?" He had invested heavily in these people, and now they were bolting and breaking his heart as they left.

Let's face it; we live in a low trust society. People do not trust politicians, physicians, parents, and pastors. Due to the exponential increase in the divorce rate, a dysfunctional upbringing, as well as being disappointed by public figures, people are extremely skeptical these days of anyone in the role of leadership. They have trust issues when it comes to church leadership. People are bringing a lot of suspicion with them to church. Perhaps it's from their family of origin, a previous bad experience in another church, or from continuous scandals that are made public; people have trouble trusting leaders.

The Factors of Trust

As part of a research project, I surveyed hundreds of people in various churches to find out the reasons people have such a challenge trusting their leaders. Two main factors repeatedly surfaced.

When asked if a person's family of origin has an impact on his/her trust of current church leaders, 80.8% said it strongly affects trust. This same group was asked if a person's previous church experience has an impact on his/her capacity to trust current church leaders. 87% of people said it strongly or somewhat strongly affects trust. I discovered there was no time limit on this previous experience. If a person had a bad experience twenty years ago where trust was broken, it still had an impact on his or her ability to trust today.

I believe every person you lead possesses a trust fund. What you do and say can cause people to make deposits or withdrawals into that trust fund. In this chapter, we want to look at the things that both build and break trust, and how we can develop practices that will make deposits into our trust fund. We will also focus on how trust is essential on any leadership team.

The Foundation of Trust

When we talk about trust, what do we mean? The dictionary defines trust as "to have confidence in, to rely upon, to respect, to be willing to follow."[1] We can look at this definition on two levels: In relation to our trust in God and secondly, believing others in our life.

First, trust is the foundation of our faith. We are instructed multiple times in the Scriptures to trust the Lord. *"Commit your way to the LORD; trust in him and he will do it."* (Psalm 37:5, NASB)

"Trust in the LORD with all your heart; do not depend on your own understanding. Seek his will in all you do, and he will show you which path to take." (Proverbs 3:5-6) *"Do not let your heart be troubled. Trust in God, trust also in me."* (John 14:1) Trusting in the Lord is the core of Christianity. What makes us believers is believing. We believe in the finished work of Jesus Christ. Trust in God's leaders is also important. It is amazing to me that people who have no difficulty trusting God can, at the same time, have little or no trust in God's leaders. Those who follow Jesus Christ may find it problematic to follow those who care for and protect Christ's Church.

Can you imagine someone saying to you, I trust you, I want to spend time with you, but I don't like your wife? I don't mind talking to you, but I will avoid and loathe your wife. I want to have a friendship with you, but don't ask me to be supportive of your spouse in any way.

People do that with Christ and His bride, the church. They say, I want to have a relationship with You Jesus; I trust You, but don't ask me to trust Your Bride the church. I will avoid it, keep my distance, and look for those in leadership to fail at some level so that it can reinforce my belief that church leaders cannot be trusted.

My wife shared a quote with me recently that has stuck in my memory. It says, "If being hurt by church causes you to lose faith in God, then your faith is in people not in God."

Is it possible for congregants to trust their leaders and leaders to trust their followers? Let's look at what it will take on our part as leaders to build our trust fund with people.

It is important to make a distinction here. We are not talking about blind trust. I am not encouraging or promoting that people blindly trust their leaders and that leaders blindly trust their followers. What I am referring to is what is called "smart trust."

"Smart trust is the ability to extend trust wisely in a world that seems to be saying you can't trust anyone."[2] As Ronald Reagan once said, "Trust, but verify."[3]

This type of trust can help people differentiate between those who have wounded them and current leadership. He or she does not lump all leaders together but can trust each individually and learn to trust them while using discernment. So let's take a look at those things that build this kind of trust.

The Feature of Trust

Throughout the Bible, trust is seen as an essential quality of a leader. Here are just a few of the many passages mentioning the importance of trust:

"But select capable men from all the people, men who fear God, trustworthy men who hate dishonest gain and appoint them as officials over thousands, hundreds, fifties, and tens." (Exodus 18: 21, N.I.V.)

"They rose early in the morning and went out to the wilderness of Tekoa; and when they went out, Jehoshaphat stood and said, 'Listen to me, O Judah and inhabitants of Jerusalem, put your trust in the LORD your God, and you will be established. Put your trust in His prophets *and you will succeed.'"* (2 Chronicles 20:20, N.A.S.B.)

"It is required of a steward that one be found trustworthy," (1 Corinthians 4:2, N.A.S.B.)

"Now we ask you, brothers, to respect those who work hard among you, who are over you in the Lord and admonish you, and to esteem them very highly in love because of their work. Be at peace among yourselves." (1 Thessalonians 5:12-13, E.S.V.)

The Formation of Trust

How is trust built? How do we make deposits into our trust fund? Here are some things that can increase our integrity with people:

1. *Character-* When leaders are transparent, humble, vulnerable, and growing in spiritual maturity and Christlikeness, trust rises. This does not mean that leaders are perfect; it does mean that they are humble enough to admit they are not.
2. *Consistency-* When leaders keep their commitments, follow through on appointments, keep their word and are honest, they are exercising behaviors that enhance their leadership leverage. Leaders practice consistency in their conduct. They are not one way with one group of people and different way with another. They are consistent in their conversation.
3. *Caring-* Leaders who show respect and demonstrate concern for their followers find their trust temperature rising. John Maxwell says, "People don't care how much you know until they know how much you care."[4] Perceived care is an important factor in building trust.
4. *Communication-* This involves communicating change, listening empathetically, and speaking honestly. It also means making sure those who are impacted by a decision are informed when a decision is made
5. *Competency-* This means being skilled at doing one's job well, being teachable and continually seeking to sharpen one's skills.

In surveying people, I discovered that doing one's job well scored the lowest of the qualities needed to build trust. It appears that character, consistency, caring, and communication were more important to people in whether they could trust their leader than doing a good job. This does not mean that a person should not work hard and know what they are doing; it means there are things that are more important to people in the long run when it comes to increasing trust.

The Fracturing of Trust

Let's now look at the flipside and see what causes the trust to diminish. Here are some of the things that can cause withdrawals from our trust fund:

1. *Dishonesty-* When people feel lied to or deceived, they break their trust. When they are told one thing and then treated differently, they find it difficult to trust their leader. The challenge of this is that even the perception of dishonesty can cause diminishing trust. We will look more closely at this when we talk about resolving a conflict, but even a misperception by someone can create a chasm in his or her trust.
2. *Pride-* When a leader is defensive, refusing to validate another person, or when they believe that it's their way or the highway, people stop following. There is a fine line between arrogance and confidence as a leader. Arrogance is based on self-reliance; confidence is based on God's presence with one as he or she leads.
3. *Lack of Concern-* When someone's input is not valued, or he or she is shown a lack of respect, people have trouble trusting. When people feel used or manipulated, they stop trusting their leaders. When leaders practice neglect, they become suspect!
4. *Lack of Communication-* Rick Warren says, "people are down on what they are not up on." If people don't know what is going on, they will struggle to follow. If they feel a lack of respect by not being communicated with,

particularly when the change impacts them, they will withdraw from your trust fund.

Again, the leadership challenge is that despite our best efforts to communicate, some people are looking for a reason not to trust. You can relate to people in various ways, and they still may respond in this manner. It has been proven that people need eight exposures to information before they begin to understand and remember it. A friend once said to me, "just at the time you are getting sick of talking about something is right around the time your people are just beginning to understand it."

5. *Lack of Competency-* When people feel that the leader is not capable of leading effectively, they will withhold trust. When leaders drop the ball and do a poor job of planning or equipping people, trust becomes a casualty.

Stephen M.R. Covey says that when trust breaks down, the speed of decision-making grinds to a halt. He says, "Low trust is the greatest cost in life and in organizations, including families. Low trust creates hidden agendas, politics, interpersonal conflict, interdepartmental rivalries, win-lose thinking, defensive and protective communication-all which reduce the speed of trust. Low trust slows everything-every decision, every communication, and every relationship"[4] If the area that we are leading is to be healthy and accomplish its intended results, we need to focus on the trust temperature of the organization.

He makes some helpful distinctions between a high and low trust organization.

Here are the characteristics of a high trust organization:
- Information is shared quickly and openly.
- Mistakes are expected.

- There is a collaborative spirit.
- Members share the credit.
- There is loyalty.
- There is honesty and vulnerability.
- Communication about decision-making is communicated clearly as to why and how the decisions are made.
- Input is welcomed.
- Feedback for the sake of improvement is pursued.
- Clarifying before concluding is practiced.

Contrast that to a low-trust organization:

- People manipulate information and withhold ideas.
- They seek to defend their turf.
- They become experts at spinning information.
- There is a lot of blaming and accusing.
- There is a lot of water cooler talk.
- There are meetings after the meeting.
- Certain topics are considered not discussable.
- There is little energy and low engagement.[5]

The Flow of Trust

In order for a church or organization to be healthy and have a high degree of trust, the flow of trust needs to move in four directions. I call this, the 360 degrees of trust.

There must be a downward flow, (leaders to followers) a lateral flow (peer to peer), an upward flow (followers to leaders) and personal flow. (Inside out) If an organization is lacking in one of these areas, the trust temperature will decrease. For a helpful tool in measuring your church on all four of these areas, go to www.leadershipforlifebook.com

As the pastor at the beginning of this chapter continued to share with me about what that long time member said to him, it became apparent that this person no longer felt cared for, and somehow communication had become faulty. The church had grown, and these members no longer felt important or needed. The pastor appeared detached and disinterested in them.

I encouraged this church leader to look at these two areas, caring and communication, and how he could seek to improve them in the future. It may be that the relationship is beyond repair, but at least he can prevent future breaches of trust.

As a leader, you will deal with the ebb and flow of trust on an on-going basis. Having some tools in your toolbox can help you assess and enhance your trust level in your leadership, and can be extremely beneficial.

Talk it Over:

1. What makes it difficult for you to trust others?

2. Which of the above-mentioned trust builders is most important to you?

3. As you look at your current leadership team, which of the five trust builders is the strongest? Which of these needs developing?

Going Deeper:

Covey, Stephen M.R. *The Speed of Trust*. New York: Free Press, 2006.

Horsager, David. *The Trust Edge: How Top Leaders Gain Faster Results, Deeper Relationships and a Stronger Bottom Line*. New York: Free Press, 2009.

Chapter 4

Leading with a Towel

"*Great Leaders must become Great Servants.*"
Robert Greenleaf

One of my favorite television shows is "Undercover Boss." Whenever I watch the show using the filter of leadership, I learn countless lessons. It is the only program I watch with a pen and paper nearby to record insights. In each episode, the CEO of a company dons a disguise and goes undercover at one of his or her franchises. He or she interacts with workers and learns what is working and what needs improving. The leader listens to people's stories and learns their personal history.

One of the guiding principles of each segment of the show is the principle of incarnational servant leadership. The power of the show is when a leader serves his people; the CEO becomes more understanding and the employees more loyal. Sometimes these bosses also become frustrated by what they discover as they do life alongside their employees.

In our world today, we measure the effectiveness of a leader by his or her education, charisma, power or control, and appearance. We conclude that because a person has a winsome personality, he or she is worthy of following. The bottom line in our world is results. It doesn't matter how you treat people as long as you get the results you want. We esteem these virtues in someone making his or her way to the top.

Jesus turned the power scale upside down when He walked the Earth. During His ministry, Jesus presented a revolutionary principle for His time. It is still a radical idea today.

"Jesus called them together and said, 'You know the rulers of the Gentiles lord it over them, and their high officials exercise authority over them. Not so with you. Instead, whoever wants to become great among you must be your servant, and whoever wants to be first must be your slave- just as the Son of Man did not come to be served, but to serve, and to give his life as a ransom for many.'" (Matthew 20:25-28)

Jesus said that to be effective leaders of His church, we must have a servant's heart.

Years ago, I heard Pastor Stuart Briscoe preach that there are three words for servant in the New Testament for the word servant. The first is the word "diakonos." We get our word deacon or deaconess from this word. This word us used twenty-nine times in the New Testament, to describe a person's *work*. Paul used this word frequently; he described the leader, *"He has enabled us to be ministers of his new covenant. This is a covenant not of written laws, but of the Spirit."* (2 Corinthians 3:6.) As a "diakonos," we are to be diligent in our serving others, not complacent. What does it mean to you to serve diligently?

This word is also used to describe a title of a church leader. In addition to elders, deacons and deaconesses would be selected to help lead God's church. In many church settings these people have the responsibility for the physical aspects of the church, while the elders take care of the ministry of the Word and prayer. (See Acts 6)

A second word that is used even more frequently is the word "doulos." This word means "bond-servant" and describes the relationship of the slave to his master. This word is used 119 times in the New Testament. During biblical times, a bondservant had to surrender his rights for the sake of his master. This word implies God's calling on our life. The Apostle Paul found his identity as a "bond-servant" of Christ. He frequently opened his letters to the churches identifying himself as a "doulos" of Jesus Christ. He learned that his number one goal was to serve God and Him alone. *"Am I now trying to win the approval of men, or of God? Or am I trying to please men? If I were trying to please men, I would not be a* <u>servant</u> *of Christ."* (Galatians 1:10)

This word "doulos" has to do with our *attitude*. A bond-servant would lay aside his rights, position, and perks and take up his responsibilities to love and serve others. Paul put it this way, *"Don't look out only for your own interests, but take an interest in others, too. You must have the same attitude that Christ Jesus had. Though he was God, he did not think of equality with God as something to cling to. Instead, he gave up his divine privileges; he took the humble position of a 'doulos' and was born as a human being."* (Philippians 2:4-7)

Jesus laid aside the perks of paradise and humbled Himself like no other by being born in poverty and by natural childbirth. He could have come riding into town on the back of a white steed, making His way to a palace, but instead, He embodied servanthood for His followers.

The final word for a servant in the New Testament is the word "hyperetes." This word literally means "under-rower." This term is used twenty times in the New Testament. In classical Greek, ships would set course by sail. But when the winds died down, the under-rowers would go to work. Below the boat, a group of servants that would pull on the oars. Their leader would stand above them on a pedestal giving the cadence and the speed at which they were to row. The captain would also set the course and the direction.

We are "under-rowers" for Christ. As God's servants, we are called upon to pull on the oars. He is the one who sets the speed and the direction, where to go, when to go and how fast. The keyword for a "hyperetes" is faithfulness. This word describes our *commitment*. When Christ tells us to row, we need to be faithful in following His direction. Luke used this word to describe himself and others who helped him compile the account of Jesus' life; *"just as those who from the beginning were eyewitnesses and "hyperetes" of the word have delivered them to us."* (Luke 1:2 ESV.)

What Makes a Good Servant Leader?

Now that we have a better understanding of what a servant is and does, let's look at some of the character qualities of a servant leader in the Bible. How does he or she differ from a secular leader? What does the Bible have to say about the leaders as a servant? Here are some things I have discovered:

1. *A servant leader values people.* An effective leader sees the value in everyone from the top of the organizational chart to the bottom. As Christian leaders, we see a person's value because of how much he or she means to Christ. If leaders don't value people, they won't serve them. If we begin to see people as equipment to get a job done, we will soon cease serving them. Paul said, *"Don't look out only for your own interests, but take an interest in others, too."* Philippians 2:4

2. *A servant leader models what they want to be done.* Jesus, the Master-servant, gave us an amazing example of this principle. On the night He was betrayed, knowing what lie ahead for Him, knowing that all of His followers

would forsake Him, knowing that He would be beaten, ridiculed, falsely accused and abandoned, He took up a towel and washed the disciple's feet. After doing so, He told them to do the same to one another. (John 13:14-16) Servant leaders must model to others what they want done. No task is below them.

3. *A servant leader goes the extra mile.*–A respected leader does what he or she can to help others in their time of need. He or she will not settle for the minimum, but instead will seek to exceed a person's expectations when it comes to serving.

4. *A servant leader approaches life with humility-* A servant leader realizes that he or she can learn from others and receive input from them as well. He is teachable. A servant leader can receive instruction from anyone.

5. *A servant leader is a secure leader-* If you are going to serve others; you need to know whom you are and why you are doing what you are doing. You will need to learn to be okay with others getting the credit or getting the applause. You must realize that you are ultimately living your life for an audience of One.

Servant leaders have enough self-assurance and inner strength that they know who they are and what they are capable of doing. In other words, they understand their uniqueness as a leader and they don't fear losing their position. They don't naively allow unscrupulous people to take over, but they don't worry about their status or title being taken away either.

6. *A servant leader knows his or her limits-* An authentic leader does not attempt to assume the role of God or the Holy Spirit in another person's life. He or she realizes his or her limits and accepts them. Jesus, the prime example of leadership, was not always available to serve, nor was

He always present to help with every need. Sometimes you can only do for a few what you wished you could do for many. But when you do it unto the least of these, you do it unto Him.

7. *A servant leader takes risks-* Servant leaders take the risk of being misunderstood, taken advantage of, mistreated and criticized. The reality is that you may invest a lot of time and effort in serving others only to have them turn on you and attack you. Regardless of the risks, a servant leader's greatest desire is to imitate Jesus, and therefore, to serve as Jesus did.

In an episode of "Undercover Boss," Chris McCann, an executive with "1-800-FLOWERS," goes undercover at several of his franchises. His company owns a nationwide floral business, but also a candy manufacturer as well as several other subsidiaries.

As he assumes the role of a servant, he is both excited and frustrated by what he discovers. Some of his employees truly love serving others and helping brighten people's lives by what they do. He sees some who love their job so much they are willing to pay out of their pocket to better their skills as a florist.

At another location he encounters managers being given performance goals with no input on how those goals are set, and what is realistic with the manpower they currently employ. He talks with people who don't like their job and complain to him about the lack of morale. Chris must listen without reacting and blowing his cover.

In a closing scene of this episode, Chris calls his regional managers and several employees together and makes a commitment to them to be more thoughtful and aware as the CEO of the company. In a sense, he is making a commitment to be more of a servant leader and to listen and help assist those who work for him. No wonder "1-800-FLOWERS" continues its upward trajectory in the marketplace.[1]

Talk it Over:

1. Why is serving others such a challenge?

2. Do you tend to serve people out of obligation or as an opportunity to serve Jesus?

3. Who in your opinion is a great example of a servant leader?

4. How can you practice being a servant this week?

Going Deeper:

Blanchard, Ken and Phil Hodges. *Lead Like Jesus: Lessons From the Greatest Leadership Role Model of All Time*. Nashville: Thomas Nelson, 2005.

Chapter 5

Impossible or Him-possible?

"*Without faith it is impossible to please God.*"
Hebrews 11:6- N.I.V.

The story is told of two nuns who worked at the local hospital. One day on their way to work they ran out of gas. They had no gas can so they searched around and found a bedpan in the back seat. In their robes and habits, they walked to a nearby gas station and filled the bedpan with gas. They returned to their car and began pouring the gas into the tank. As they poured, a passing driver noticed them and pulled up alongside of them and rolled his window down. Looking at the bedpan they were using to pour the gasoline, he said, "Now that is real faith!" In this chapter, we want to discover what real faith looks like.

One of the most important qualities of a leader is his or her personal faith. Having faith in God is an incredibly important quality for a leader. God's Word says, "*And it is impossible to please God without faith. Anyone who wants to come to him must believe that God exists and that he rewards those who sincerely seek him.*" (Hebrews 11:6)

Why is it so important for a leader to possess tremendous faith? As a leader, it's difficult to pass along what you don't possess. Notice I did not say impossible. You can impart seeds of faith to your followers that they can take and grow with God's help beyond you and your leadership.

Leaders, however, are meant to be examples to their followers when times get rough. They are the ones who lead the way. Max Lucado says, "Faith is not the belief that God will do what you want; faith is the belief that God will do what is right."[1]

Before we look at what genuine faith looks like, let's take a look at what the Bible says is the opposite of faith. Before we can see what the real thing looks like, we have to see some counterfeits.

The Opposite of Faith

We would probably all agree that *fear is the opposite of faith.* Fear causes us to shrink back while faith challenges us to move forward. The people of God in the Old Testament were camped at the edge of the land He promised to them. The only thing left to do was to send in a group of spies to do a reconnaissance mission to determine how they would attack. They spent forty days spying out the land.

Upon returning, the majority gave a report filled with fear. They said, *"the people living there are powerful, and their towns are large and fortified. We even saw giants there, the descendants of Anak! Next to them we felt like grasshoppers, and that's what they thought too!* (Numbers 13: 28,33) Instead of listening to the two spies who saw the situation with faith in a God who had led his people out of Egypt, parted the Red Sea, provided manna and quail for them in the wilderness and supplied water from a rock, the people listened to their fears and refused to move forward. The result was disastrous. That's why forty years later, when God once again told them to enter the land, He told Joshua, three times, *"Be strong and courageous! Do not be afraid or discouraged. For the LORD, your God is with you wherever you go."* (Joshua 1:9) It has been said, "Courage is not the absence of fear, it is doing the right thing in spite of those fears."[2] A further contrast to faith is *living by what we see*. To live by faith, we must resist the temptation to look around at what others may or may not be doing, and instead keep our eyes focused on Christ and His kingdom agenda. As a leader, you will continually fight between keeping on eye on where you are now and where you need to go in the future. If we focus too much on the now, we may live in fear of what might happen. If we live too much in the future, we may neglect the steps of faith needed to get us there. The Apostle Paul said, *"We live by faith and not by sight."* (2 Corinthians 5:7) It is important keep to looking ahead. While dealing with the "what ifs" is an important part of leadership, we must supersede them with thoughts that "God will."

The third counterpart to living by faith is *living in our own strength*. The Bible tells us that the *"...And the Spirit gives us desires that are opposite of what the sinful nature desires. These two forces are constantly fighting against each other, so you are not free to carry out your good intentions."* (Galatians 5:17) When I live in the flesh, the fallen part of me, I am not living by faith. How do I know when I have crossed the line? What are some indicators that I am now listening to my flesh rather than living by faith? In Galatians 5, Paul shares with us some signs of life in the flesh:

- When I become habitually critical of people- Galatians 5:15
- When I become self-centered, making it all about me- Galatians 5:13
- When I am continually frustrated with people and experiencing multiple conflicts in my life.–Galatians 5:20

- When I find myself using substitutes to medicate the pain in my life- Galatians 5:19-21

The final contrast to faith found in God's Word is *unbelief*. Unbelief is different than having honest questions and even doubts at times. John the Baptist, the cousin of Jesus, is the one who proclaimed, *"Behold the Lamb of God that takes away the sins of the world!"* (John 1:29) After his arrest, John had doubts that Jesus was truly the Messiah, and sent some of his friends to ask him if he was indeed the Chosen One.

Unbelief is refusing to believe that God can and will do what He has promised. The Apostle James says,

"If you need wisdom, ask our generous God, and he will give it to you. He will not rebuke you for asking. But when you ask him, be sure that your faith is in God alone. Do not waver, for a person with divided loyalty is unsettled as a wave of the sea that is blown and tossed by the wind. Such people should not expect to receive anything from the Lord. Their loyalty is divided between God and the world, and they are unstable in everything the do." (James 1:5-8)

What Faith Looks Like

To begin looking at what true faith looks like, it's important to understand the nature of faith. Faith has both a *present* and *future* element to it. Presently, faith is applying and obeying what I know to be true about God to my life. The future aspect of faith is trusting God to fulfill His plan for my life and ministry. If you are not practicing the present element of faith, it is impossible to expect God to lead you into the future.

At the John G. Shedd Aquarium in Chicago, you will find a most unusual type of fish known as the Anablep. These sea creatures are very unique. Their eyes are divided into two parts giving them two sets of eyes. This is one creature you can truly call four eyes. One set of eyes sees above the water for predators, and one set sees below the surface of the water for its prey. As a leader, we often need to have our faith focused like the Anableps. We need to focus on our current reality, as well as trust God for the future. The key is having faith. It involves obeying now and trusting God for a grand future.

Secondly, it's important to understand that the key to faith is not the *amount* of faith we have, but who is the *object* of our faith. Jesus told us that if we had the amount of faith equal to a mustard seed, we could see miracles happen. (Luke 17:3-6) The Apostle Paul wrote to the believers in Galatia, *"My old self has been crucified with Christ. It is no longer I who live, but Christ lives in me. So I live in this earthly body by trusting in the Son of God, who loved me and gave himself for me."* (Galatians 2:20) The writer of Hebrews said, *"And let us run with endurance the race God has set before us. We do this by keeping our eyes on Jesus, the champion who initiates and perfects our faith."* (Hebrews 12:2) The most important thing about our faith is our focus, not on faith itself, but the object of our faith, Jesus Christ.

We also grow in our faith in Christ by getting into God's Word. The more we discover the greatness of God, the more our faith in Him grows and develops. Again, Paul helps us understand what faith is when he writes, *"So faith comes from hearing, that is, hearing the Good News about Christ."* (Romans 10:17) Our faith also grows and strengthens as we spend time in personal worship. David wrote, *"I will praise you forever, O God, I will trust in your good name in the presence of your faithful people."* (Psalm 52:9) It is important to understand that we do not worship the Word; we worship the God of the Word. When you open your Bible, God opens His mouth and begins to reveal who He is to us. The result is that we grow in faith.

Furthermore, faith is an active belief that God will accomplish His plan for my life and my leadership. Faith is a verb, not a noun. It involves taking a step and trusting that God will be there to provide. *"The one who calls you is faithful, and he will do it."* (1 Thessalonians 5:24)

Faith is often grown during problems, pressure and pain. Faith requires us to trust God for things we cannot see or feel and to believe that He has our best in mind. C. S. Lewis wrote, "God whispers to us in our pleasures, speaks in our conscience, but shouts in our pains: it is his megaphone to rouse a deaf world." [3]

Our faith is strengthened when there is resistance, just like muscles grow stronger by utilizing a resistant force. God tells us that through difficulty, we have an opportunity to trust Him and in the process of doing so, our character is developed. (James 1:2-4)

Furthermore, you can't have faith without prayer. Our faith in God is strengthened through prayer. As a matter of fact, if you want to know how your faith is doing, take a look at your prayer life. God's Word tells us we need to ask in faith believing that God will answer. (James 1: 6-8)

Finally, let me end with one word of caution. There is a fine line between faith and foolishness. Over the years, I have seen many leaders cross this line by disguising their agenda as faith in God. Foolishness is based on a person's whims or will and usually is designed to make the person look good. Faith, on the other hand, is centered on the plan and purposes of God. It is intended to make Jesus and His kingdom look good.

Not every idea or thought comes from God. There are times we will need to ask ourselves, how much time have I spent seeking God in this matter? Not every book you read is a leading from God. Not every conference you go to is God's will for you and your church. You need to seek what God has in mind for your unique leadership context. Then step out in faith believing that God is present with you through it all. So how is your faith factor? Where do you need some faith fortification? Where is your faith faltering? What is one thing you can do today to grow stronger in your faith as a leader? Why not spend a few moments talking to God about it?

Talk it Over:

1. Why is it critical for a spiritual leader to possess great faith in God?

2. When have you seen faith cross the line into foolishness? How can you as a leader prevent that from happening?

3. In what areas of your leadership can you ask God to increase your faith in Him?

Going Deeper:

Lucado, Max. *He Still Moves Stone*. Nashville: Thomas Nelson, 2013.

Ortberg, John. *If You Want to Walk on Water, You've Got to Get Out of the Boat*. Grand Rapids: Zondervan, 2014.

Smith, Chuck. *Faith*. Costa Mesa: Word for Today, 2010.

Chapter 6

"Clean the Fuel Injectors"

"God blesses those whose hearts are pure,
for they will see God."
Matthew 5:8

When our kids were younger, we purchased a van to fit all five children in at the same time. Shortly after buying this beast, the check engine light came on. I took it back to the shop, but a few months later the same indicator light appeared. On one of my last visits, a mechanic told me that the next time it happens, add some fuel injector cleaner to the gas tank. if it goes off, then you need to continue to add it after several thousand miles of driving. Sure enough, the problem was solved. Apparently, that make and model of van was notorious for getting the fuel injectors clogged and eventually causing the engine to lose power.

The same can happen in the lives of spiritual leaders if we are not careful. Unresolved conflict, unconfessed sin, undealt with resentment and frustration can build up to a point where the power of God is unable to flow through us. We may be busy, but we are barren. The warning lights begin to appear in our emotions, our thinking, our words, and behavior.

Unattended, it can lead to major problems in our relationships and our ministry.

I once heard a professor make a statement that I wrestled with for years. After spending decades both training and working with leaders, I have come to the conclusion that he was profoundly correct. After seeing friends, leaders I respect, and members in my church crash and burn, I couldn't agree with him more. He said, "Sin will limit our service for God." I thought, no, that can't be true, God uses sinners!

His power is made perfect in our weakness. If sin limits our service for God, how can anyone qualify for ministry?

Jesus made this statement; *"God blesses those whose hearts are pure, for they will see God."* (Matthew 5:8) Peter, who failed his Lord in His hour of greatest need, wrote, *"But now you must be holy in everything you do, just as God, who chose you is holy. For the Scriptures say, 'you must be holy because I am holy.'"* (1 Peter 1:15,16)

It might be good at this point to take a time-out for a quick theology lesson. Some may respond, "Hasn't Christ already made me pure?" "Do I need to worry about practicing purity in my life if Christ is the only One who can produce it?" These are great questions; let me see if I can bring some understanding.

The book of Ephesians clearly divides into two sections. The first three chapters deal with our position in Christ, and the last three deal with our practices as Christ followers. In chapter one, Paul tells us that our position before Christ is that, *"God loved us and chose us in Christ to be holy and without fault in his eyes."* (Ephesians 1:4) This is our status before God. When God looks at us, He sees Jesus, not our sin. However, on a practical, day-in and day out basis, we are far from being "holy and without fault." The life long goal of Christians is to have our practices match our position in Christ. When we choose to follow our agenda and ambitions, the Bible calls that sin. Sin, if it is allowed to linger, begins to attach itself to our hearts, and causes the blockage of God's power to flow through us.

So how do we use God's fuel injector cleaner to unclog the debris in our mind and hearts? How do we learn purity in our lives that will make us more powerful? How do we keep the warning lights from appearing in our lives and ministries?

A Path to Purity

The first step is to *surrender to God*. It is an act of willfully surrendering our lives and plans to God. Paul challenged the believers at Rome, *"And so, dear brothers and sisters, I plead with you to give your bodies to God because of all he has done for you. Let them be a living and holy sacrifice- the kind he will find acceptable. This is truly the way to worship him."* (Romans 12:1)

While some would contend that this is a one-time surrender of our lives to God, I believe it happens at a point in time, but it continues on a regular basis. As one speaker said, "the problem with living sacrifices is they keep creeping off the altar." You have to put repeatedly put them back on back on the altar.

When we come to a place of saying, "God, I can't, but You can," we are admitting we are powerless and are relying on God's power to flow through us. Those who are in recovery recognize the power of this statement. It is the first step to see God heal them from the fears, frustrations and failures in their lives.

Secondly, in order to practice purity, we need to be *filled with the Holy Spirit*. Paul wrote, *"Don't be drunk with wine because this will ruin your life. Instead, be filled with the Spirit."* (Ephesians 5:18) The word "filled" means "controlled by." It is a present tense verb that means we are to *be continually filled* with the Spirit. Notice the comparison to being drunk with wine and being filled with the Spirit. A person who is drunk is not in control of his or her life any longer. A person who is drunk will often do and say things that are not part of his or her usual character. Finally, one who is drunk with wine will often not worry about what others think, which is often a detriment to him or her.

When the Holy Spirit controls a person, he or she will also do things that are not part of his or her usual character, such as loving those who are hard to love, forgiving those who don't deserve it, and practicing kindness when opposed.

Paul tells the church at Galatia that when the Holy Spirit controls us, we will produce the fruit of the Spirit. These fruit are the kinds of behaviors that produce purity in our lives. He writes, *"But the Holy Spirit produces this kind of fruit in our lives: love, joy, peace, patience, kindness, goodness, faithfulness, gentleness, and self-control."* (Galatians 5:22-23) When I look at this list, I quickly realize that I cannot produce these kinds of behaviors on my own. Only as I surrender and Christ controls me can I see these outcomes begin to happen.

One more thing, it's important to understand that while this fruit all comes from the same source, it may not all grow at the same rate. Some of these qualities are more in need of developing than others in the life of a leader. What's most important is to take an inventory of your life from time to time and ask; "How am I doing in each of these behaviors?" Ask yourself; "Am I growing?" "Is there an area I need to ask the Holy Spirit to develop in me?" If you are like me, you can find a few areas you need Christ to cultivate in your life.

Furthermore, there is another method for producing purity in our lives, one that you may have not realized. It's something I have resisted in my life, yet I have seen its profound impact in producing Christ-like character and in pruning my selfish tendencies. *It is suffering.* Peter writes, *"These trials will show that your faith is genuine. It is being tested as fire tests and purifies gold- though your faith is far more precious than mere gold."* (1 Peter 1:7) God can purify our character by refining our lives in the furnace of affliction. He melts away the impurities when we go through times of trials. While God uses pain and difficulty to purify hearts, He always has His hand on the thermostat. He knows when enough is enough, and will, in His time, bring us through the season of suffering, stronger and more mature than we were before. God doesn't want to waste a hurt in our lives.

A fourth way to promote purity in our lives is by spending time in the presence of *a Holy God.* Isaiah experienced just that when he saw the LORD, seated on a lofty throne. He witnessed angels calling out to each other, *"Holy, holy, holy is the LORD of Heaven's Armies! The whole earth is filled with is glory!"* (Isaiah 6:3) Isaiah's response was that he felt doomed, *"for I am a sinful man. I have filthy lips… Yet I have seen the King, the LORD of Heaven's Armies."* Then one of the angels took a burning coal from the altar and touched Isaiah's lips and with it, and said; *"Now your guilt is removed, and your sins are forgiven."* (Isaiah 6:7) After experiencing this forgiveness, Isaiah then heard the LORD asking, *"Whom should I send as a messenger to this people? Who will go for us?* Isaiah responded, *"Here I am. Send me."* (Isaiah 6:8)

Where I live, it's not unusual for the temperature outside to be warm enough to get a suntan, or in my case, a good sunpinking. You can usually tell when a person has been in the sun. Their face and features reflect the glow. They don't even need to say where they have been; and it is obvious that they have been spending time outdoors in contact with the sun.

The same is true of God's people. If we spend time in God's presence, to the Son, our faces and features will reflect it. People will notice that we have been with Jesus. People will begin to see the difference in our lives even before we speak a word that something is different about our life. Just as Moses went up into the presence of the LORD and had to put a veil over his face to not frighten the people of God, Paul tells us, *"So all of us who have had that veil removed can see and reflect the glory of the Lord. And the LORD-who is the Spirit-makes us more and more like him as we are changed into his glorious image."* (2 Corinthians 3:18)

A final way to produce purity in our lives is *by getting into God's Word, the Bible.* Jesus' prayer for His disciples and those who would follow after them is found in John 17. Part of Jesus prayer to the Father was, *"make them holy by your truth; teach them your word, which is truth."* (John 17:17) When we get into God's Word, or better yet, get God's Word into us, our minds are renewed, our will is realigned, our emotions are reframed and our spirit refreshed. We are reminded of God's plan and purpose for our lives.

As I close this chapter, I encourage you to take an inventory of your life right now. Is there anything that is steering you away from purity in your life? Is there addiction? Is there an unhealthy practice that is clogging up the power source of your life? Do you find the desire for purity in your life less than a passionate pursuit?

I want to encourage you to do two things. First, confess it to God. I once heard a speaker say, "Confession is naming reality." It is acknowledging the problem and agreeing with God and yourself that you are powerless to overcome this on your own.

The Apostle John wrote, *"If we claim we have no sin, we are only fooling ourselves and not living in the truth. But if we confess our sins to him, he is faithful and just to forgive our sins and to cleanse us from all wickedness."* (1 John 1:8-9)

The second thing is *to make yourself accountable to at least one other person.* As Rick Warren says, "you are only as sick as your secrets." When we confess our sin to at least one other person, the power of that destructive sin is broken. James writes, *"Confess your sins to each other and pray for each other so that you may be healed."* (James 5:16)

I pray that you will not quickly gloss over this chapter and move onto the next. I have seen too many of my friends and colleagues have to remove themselves from leadership because they didn't take the time to ask the tough questions about purity. The little things soon became big, and the momentum of addiction was so strong that there was no turning back. The result was significant devastation to their family, their ministry, and to those who followed their leadership. I pray that God will impress upon you the importance of these words and take them to heart because purity brings God's power!

Talk it Over:

1. What makes the practice of purity such a challenge for leaders today?

2. Why is personal holiness not addressed a lot today?

3. What area mentioned in this chapter will you practice beginning today?

Going Deeper:

Bridges, Jerry. *The Pursuit of Holiness: Run in Such a Way as to Get the Prize, 1 Corinthians 9:24*. Colorado Springs: Navpress, 2006.
Ingram, Chip. *True Spirituality*. New York: Howard Books, 2013.

Chapter 7

Growth Spurts

"Growth happens at the edge of your comfort zone!"
Jim Hanna

Y ears ago when we bought our house, we discovered
several things we didn't expect. Things like unreported
water damage and a lawsuit against the builder of the home
concerning the windows leaking were just some of the frustrations. There was one thing, however, that gave us a chuckle.
In one of the closets, on the backside of the door were pencil
marks. These were at different heights with initials on them.
Apparently, the previous owners took the time to measure
their children's growth and record it on the backside of the
closet door. That way their children could see how much they
had grown since the last measurement.

I wish we had a similar system for measuring our growth
as leaders, some way that we could, with a quick glance, see
that we have grown six inches in the Lord in the past year.
We could also see if we had plateaued at all.

As a leader, it is crucial to recognize and monitor your
personal growth. You cannot lead people further than you
have gone yourself. You also cannot impart what you do not
possess. The greatest contribution that you can make to those

you lead is your continual growth. You cannot lead others until you have learned to lead yourself.

Personal growth as a leader is not automatic. You cannot rely solely on your giftedness, abilities and personality. There must be a deliberate, intentional and consistent plan of action. It doesn't mean that you won't get sidetracked or have setbacks; it means, that your growth as a spiritual leader is intentional, not random.

Amy Carmichael once wrote:

> "Sometimes when we read the words of those who have been more than conquerors, we feel almost despondent. I feel that I shall never be like that. But they won through step by step, by little bits of will, little denials of self, little inward victories, by faithfulness in very little things. They became who they are. No one sees these little hidden steps. They only see the accomplishments; but even so, those small steps were taken. This is no sudden triumph. There is no spiritual maturity that is the work of the moment."[1]

In this chapter, I want to look at several areas of growth. If someone were to ask you, what are you doing to grow spiritually? how would you answer? Would you be able to articulate your plan for Bible intake, prayer, connecting in a biblical community, serving and sharing? In this book, I have attempted to emphasize that the greatest leadership book you can read is God's Word. Are you reading God's Word to get to know Him better or just to prepare a teaching lesson? Anything you can do to allow God's Word to settle down and makes its home in your heart, mind and actions is well worth the investment. I would encourage you not to get hung up on the routine you may or may not use, but rather focus on the relationship that God wants to have with you.

Our pastor has implemented something recently that has been great. After a quick stand-up meeting to begin our day where we share what we will be doing for the day, as well as any prayer requests, he then challenges us to spend the next fifteen minutes in quiet time with the Lord. He feels it is so important for our staff to serve out of the "being" that he has us start our day focusing on it.

Not everyone has this luxury. Maybe for you this means getting to work fifteen minutes early and sitting in your car and spending some time with the Lord. Maybe it means taking the time to pray during your commute or at your lunch break.

Another important area in which to have a growth plan is emotional growth. Many Christian leaders begin to serve the Lord but have never learned how to process their emotions in a healthy way. Consequently, when the chips are down, they react out of their emotions rather than respond biblically.

There are many great resources on emotional health. Peter Scazzero has written several excellent books on this topic including *"Emotionally Healthy Spirituality"* and *"The Emotionally Healthy Leader,"* both of which I highly recommend.

In this chapter, I would like to focus on a couple of areas on emotional health that leaders need to monitor on a consistent basis. The first is learning to identify and process our emotions. As leaders, we can use busyness as a way of avoiding processing our frustrations. Doing so can lead us into all kinds of unhealthy practices. It is critical that a leader take the time to process his emotions to avoid damage to his leadership effectiveness.

Chip Ingram says in his book, *Overcoming Emotions that Destroy*, that there are three kinds of people when it comes to expressing our emotions. There are *"stuffers."* These people stuff their emotions until they can no longer deny the reality of what they are feeling. Sometimes they will turn the emotions inward and suffer from anxiety and depression. At other times, they will move to the second type of people.

These are called "spewers." These types of people are those who erupt with their emotions like a volcano and spew their pent up emotions on everyone near them. The fallout is usually damaging to those nearby.

The third type of leaders who express their emotions as "leakers." These people tend to let out the emotional hurt in a more subtle, passive-aggressive manner. They tend to be more covert in expressing their anger and frustration. Sometimes this will come out in sarcasm and criticism, other times by sabotaging someone's initiative.[2]

I would like to add a fourth kind of person to this mix. I call them "processors." These people have learned to feel their emotions but not be mastered by them. They have learned to process their hurt in a healthy way and have learned to express it in a constructive manner, not a destructive one. I would like to share with you one tool that has helped me process my emotions in a healthy way. I can't say I am perfect in this area but the following tool has helped both me and those close to me.

Every few days as part of my time alone with the Lord I take a few moments to recognize and record some of the unhealthy emotions that attempt to steal my health and joy as a leader. In the front of one of my Bible I have this acronym that I use as a template:

Learning to do a H.E.A.R.T. check

H- Where am I hurting? Have I been wounded lately?

E- Where am I envious? -Am I struggling with jealousy because God seems to be blessing someone else?

A- Where am I angry? What is causing the anger? What steps can I take to diffuse it?

R- am I regretful? Is there any unresolved guilt I need to deal with?

T- Where am I tense? Am I anxious?

David wrote these words as a prayer to the Lord, *"Search me, O God, and know my heart; test me and know my anxious thoughts. Point out anything in me that offends you, and lead me along the path of everlasting life."* (Psalm 139: 23-24) After doing this heart check, I take a few moments to acknowledge them to God and ask for His grace in my life in dealing with these potentially toxic emotions. As we become honest with God, those powerful emotions begin to dissolve.

Learning to Grieve

The second area of emotional growth that I have found that a leader must deal with, particularly if they have served for any length of time, are the stages of grief. The emotion of grief can come to us in numerous ways, such as having a key member abandon your leadership, an unexpected death of someone you are leading, or someone you have trusted turning on you. When we experience disappointments from seeing marriages dissolve in our church or experiencing any loss in our lives, we as leaders need to learn how to process these emotions of loss and grieve them in a healthy way.

I have taken the five stages of grief that are most well known and adapted them to help spiritual leaders learn the stages of grief. Keep in mind these phases are not sequential in nature, one after the other, but more cyclical, and people tend to move back and forth through them.

Stage # 1- *Shock and bewilderment-*What happened?
Stage # 2- *Minimizing and compartmentalizing-* Things must go on despite the loss.
Stage # 3- *Anger and questioning-* Why did this happen?

Stage # 4- *Sadness and loss-* Letting oneself feel these feelings.

Stage # 5-*Acceptance of the new normal-* Learning to adjust to life as it is now, not as it use to be.

Learning to process these phases either by recognition, recording or through the help of a counselor can help the leader to adjust so he or she doesn't self-destruct. As a leader, you will deal with grief in more ways than you realize.

A few years ago when I went through an extended time of grief over losses in my life, a friend encouraged me to write a personal "Psalm of Lament." She mentioned that several of the Psalms written included the author's pouring his heart out to God in grief. Each of these Psalms followed a pattern which can be applied to our own suffering and hurt. Here is the pattern that they followed:

1. *An Honest Address to God.* A pouring out of one's heart before God, asking Him "Where are you God?" "Why did You allow this to happen to me?"
2. *A Complaint.* Confessing your anger before God and wrestling with His will.
3. *Additional Arguments.* Is there anything else you want to say to God about your need?
4. *A Request or Petition.* What is your deepest desire from God? Often this includes a request of God to reveal Himself in a powerful way!
5. *An affirmation of Trust.* Reaffirming your faith in God and believing in Him through the seeming disaster in your life.

My Old Testament professor, Dr. Robert Alden, called these types of Psalms, "Trouble and Trust" Psalms. He mentioned that the Psalmist would often find himself in some trouble and expressed it early in the Psalm but he ended the

Psalm, by reaffirming his trust in God. (See Psalm 13, 17, 22, and 31 for examples of this.)

The third area of growth is *vocational* growth. This type of growth is growing in your areas of responsibility. This area of growth could include a reading plan, networking forums or continuing education. If funds are limited, there are some great articles as blogs that help sharpen you as a leader. One word of caution: in today's world you have to learn to be selective about what you read and to what you devote your attention. There is so much to experience on line, e-books, blogs, podcasts, webinars, etc. It is important to narrow your plan to just a few themes. By focusing on a few areas of growth, if something doesn't fit with those topics, you can refrain from participating in them.

Furthermore, another area to think intentionally about is having a discipleship growth plan. Do I have a plan to pour into the life of others? Is someone who I respect mentoring me? I once heard Howard Hendricks say, "All of us need a Paul, a Barnabas and a Timothy in our lives." He went on to explain that a Paul is someone you look up to who is older than you in the Lord and has some life experiences to share with you. A Barnabas is a peer who is an encourager, a friend or colleague, who believes the best in you, and who loves you and supports you no matter what. A Timothy is someone younger in the faith than you, someone who you are pouring into and are mentoring, a person who can learn from your life experiences.

A final area to think strategically about is to have a *family plan* for growth. As a spiritual leader, your family is the first and foremost ministry you can have. It may also be most challenging to carve out time to pay attention and supervise.

Several years ago, a friend shared with me a little formula that I have applied to both my marriage and family. I encourage you to consider something similar. It is to divert daily, withdraw weekly, maintain monthly and abandon annually.

To divert daily means I take a few moments to check in and ask how my spouse and children are doing. My wife has had a family rule since our kids were born. When we come to the dinner table, the TV goes off, no phones are allowed and no answering the phone while we are eating. We take this time to connect with each other, to talk and listen. After dinner, my wife and I spend a few minutes talking together about our day.

I realize that some families are not able to eat dinner together. In today's culture, many families are going different directions for dinner. If that is the case, then you need to be creative about your check-ins. My teenagers and young adult children respond best to text messages as a way of checking in. Others use "Facetime" or e-mail to check in.

Then there is "withdraw weekly." This means for married couples, having a regularly scheduled date night. It may mean for families having a game night or movie night with each other. Those who are single, it may mean disengaging from work and friends and spending some time with your family.

One thing my wife and I have tried to do on a weekly basis is to talk about our upcoming week. On Sunday evening, we take a few moments to discuss the next week and what we have coming up. Taking a few minutes to withdraw weekly to have a discussion like this can cure a lot of poor communication.

Also, there is "maintaining monthly." Dave Ramsey encourages couples to have a monthly meeting to balance the budget. He has found that couples that work together to develop a spending plan are well on their way to financial freedom. As a family, this may mean meeting to discuss the monthly calendar and talk about games, tournaments, and events that may be coming in the next month.

Finally, I encourage you to "abandon annually." Married couples, this means getting away, just the two of you, at least once a year together and if possible semi-annually. My wife Elizabeth and I have been married for over three decades, and we have intentionally worked to get away alone even when our five children were young. When I share this with people, some have responded, We can't afford to do that. My response to them is, Can you afford not to do this?

Abandoning annually may mean that families get away from the norm of life and the distractions to listen and learn from one another. Family vacations can be costly but there are some great deals if you will take the time to research where you are going and plan ahead.

As you reflect on this chapter and all that we have discussed, it may seem overwhelming. I would encourage you to take a piece of paper and divide into five columns. Then write at the top of the first column, "Spiritual," the second column "Emotional," then "Vocational," "Discipleship," and finally "Family/Relational." Take a few moments to list the things you have going that enhance each of these areas. Then take a moment to list some goals that you want to accomplish in the next week, month, quarter, six months or year that will help you grow in that area.

My prayer is that the tools I have shared with you in this chapter will become like the pencil marks we discovered on the back of the closet door. They will become a way to measure your growth on an ongoing basis. Wouldn't it be great to identify areas in our life that we have seen significant growth and celebrate the work God has done in our lives? Leading yourself well is the key to leading others effectively.

Talk it Over:

1. What plan do you have to grow spiritually?

2. When is the last time you did a HEART check? How did you go about it?

3. What is something you are grieving right now as a leader?

4. What plan do you have in place to grow vocationally?

5. Who is your Paul? Barnabas? Timothy?

Going Deeper:

Ingram, Chip and Becca Johnson. *Overcoming Emotions That Destroy: Practical Help for Those Angry Feeling That Ruin Relationships*. Grand Rapids: Baker Books, 2009.

Scazzero, Peter. *Emotionally Healthy Spirituality: It's Impossible to be Spiritual Mature, While Remaining Emotionally Immature*. Grand Rapids: Zondervan 2006.

Scazzero, Peter. *The Emotionally Healthy Leader: How Transforming Your Inner Life Will Deeply Transform Your Church, Team and the World*. Grand Rapids: Zondervan, 2015.

Doing a H.E.A.R.T Check
By Jim Hanna

"Search me, O God, and know my heart; test me and know my anxious thoughts. Point out anything in me that offends you, and lead me along the path of everlasting life."
Psalm 139: 23-24

H- *Where am I hurting? Have I been wounded lately?*

E- *Where am I Envious?* -Am I struggling with jealousy because God seems to be blessing someone else?

A- *Where am I angry?*

R- *Where am I regretful?* Is there any unresolved guilt I need to acknowledge?

T- *Where am I tense?* Am I anxious?

Step 2: After recognizing these emotions, take some time to confess them to God asking for His grace to process them in a healthy way.

How to Write Your Personal Psalm of Lament
By Jim Hanna

1. *An honest address to God.* A pouring out of one's heart before God, asking Him "Where are you, God?" "Why did you allow this to happen to me?"

2. *A complaint.* Confessing your anger to God and wrestling with His will.

3. *Additional arguments.* Is there anything else you want to say to God about your need?

4. *A Request or Petition.* What is your deepest desire from God? Often this includes a request of God to reveal Himself in a powerful way!

5. *An affirmation of Trust.* Reaffirming your faith in God and believing in Him through the seeming disaster in your life.

Section 2

"Influencing and Inspiring Others with Appropriate Leadership Skills"

"...And led them with skillful hands."
Psalm 78:72

Chapter 8

Listening Like a Leader

*"One of the greatest gifts you can give people
is the gift of listening."*

We have all heard the horror stories of someone not listening to someone, and in the end, paying for it. In counseling couples over the years, I have found one of the biggest causes of marital conflict is the lack of listening beyond the words to the heart of what the other person is saying. One of the skills needed to be an effective leader is the ability to listen to your followers. Without this skill, a leader can easily jump to conclusions and move too quickly in prescribing a solution without hearing the full story.

When people are heard, they feel valued. When they feel valued, they are more willing to support the leader even if they don't completely agree with him or her. In order to create ownership with those you lead, particularly when introducing change, a leader needs to listen well.

"Being heard means being taken seriously. It satisfies our need for self-expression and our need to feel connected to others. The receptive listener allows us to express what we think and feel. Hearing and acknowledging helps clarify both thoughts and feelings...The need to be known, to have our experience understood and accepted by someone who really listens, is meat and drink to the human heart." [1]

The word "listen" or "hear" is used 500 times in the Bible. In the Old Testament the word "Shama" was used when the Israelites would come together for worship. They would recite, *"Hear O Israel, the LORD your God, the LORD is One. Love the LORD your God with all your heart and with all your soul, and with all your strength."* (Deuteronomy 6:4 N.I.V.)

In the New Testament the word "listen" was used by Jesus 52 times. He would often say, *"He who has ears to hear, let them hear."* Today Jesus might say, "listen up, I have something significant to say to you."

In this chapter we will use the book of Proverbs as our guide for learning to listen as leaders. *"Too much talk leads to sin. Be sensible and keep your mouth shut."* (Proverbs 10:19) And all God's leaders said, OUCH!

Learning How to Listen like a Leader

1. *We must suspend our needs, interests and judgments.*

To take an interest in someone else, we must suspend our own. We have to learn to suspend our own agenda, forget about what we might say next, and concentrate on being a receptive listener to the other person.

This type of listening means we learn to listen to the other person without attempting to one up them or minimize what they are feeling. To listen, we cannot make the conversation about us. We need to actively and consciously work at suspending our own needs, and stay curious in order to take an interest in the other person.

"Fools have no interest in understanding; they only want to air their own opinions." (Proverbs 18:2)

2. *We must resist reacting emotionally to what the other person is saying.*

We will not be good listeners if we do not restrain the urgent need to set the other person straight or fix them. It is important to keep in mind that feelings expressed are neither right or wrong, they are simply feelings. We don't have to judge how a person feels, but rather explore why they feel the way they do.

"Spouting off before listening to the facts is both shameful and foolish." (Proverbs 18:13)

"One of the major reasons people don't listen is that they become emotionally reactive. Something in the speaker's message triggers a hurt, anger or fear that activates defensiveness and blocks understanding. Reacting emotionally to what another person says is the number one reason conversations turn into conflicts." [2]

It has been proven that when we become defensive, one thing that shuts down is our ability to listen. When our shields go up, our ears close up. No wonder the biblical writer James stated, we must be *"quick to listen, slow to speak, and slow to get angry."* (James 1:19)

A person who has demonstrated this to me is my pastor, Dave Larson. I have observed him listening non-reactively in several crucial conversations. When there has been an opportunity to respond defensively, Dave has listened empathetically to what the other person is saying. I encourage you to find someone who is a great listener and learn from them. It will save you a lot of grief in the long run.

3. *We need to remove distractions.*

We need to ask the question of each other if this is the right time and place to discuss this matter. Both should agree either formally or informally on this. Have you ever been in public and overheard someone arguing or disagreeing near you? I don't know about you, but it makes me pretty nervous. It is important if you are going to deal with important matters, that you try and find a place where you will be uninterrupted by noise or others.

Learn to ask a simple question: "Is now a good time to talk to you about something that is important to me?" By asking this, you are giving the person the freedom to either address the issue at that moment or set up a time when you can talk without distractions and interruptions.

> *"Timely advice is lovely, like golden apples*
> *in a silver basket." (Proverbs 25:11)*

4. *Avoid inappropriate responses.*

We have all been guilty of listening autobiographically. In other words we relate everything we hear to our experience. Here are some of the ways I have been guilty of responding inappropriately. Some of these responses may be conscious or sub-conscious responses.

Inappropriate Responses:

- *"I can top that"* - Translation: Your situation is nothing compared to what I have experienced. We minimize the other person's pain by comparing it to ours.
- *"That reminds me of a time…"* – Translation: Let me shift the conversation to what I am going through because what you are telling me is not that important.
- *"If I were you…"* - Translation: Let me give you a quick fix because I need you to stop bothering me.

- *"You shouldn't feel that way."* –Translation: Stop whining and get over it. You have no right to feel like this. [3]

Granted, sharing from your life may be a way of building rapport with the other person, but I caution you not to monopolize the situation with your agenda but rather listen carefully to what the other person is saying. Michael Nichols says,

> "A lot of failed listening takes the form of telling other people not to feel the way they do. The intention might be genuine, but the effect is to cheat the other person out of processing those feelings in a healthy way." [4]

An example of this in the Bible is the response of Job's friends. Upon arriving and seeing Job in his condition, they spent the next seven days in silence. They listened as Job expressed his heart and regretted even being born.

The conversation quickly shifted when they began to tell Job he shouldn't feel the way he did. They began analyzing him and diagnosing his suffering without taking the time to get the big picture.

> *"Fools think their own way is right,*
> *but the wise listen to others."*
> *(Proverbs 12:15)*

<u>Appropriate Responses:</u>

- *Ask:* "Are you saying," then paraphrase back to the person what you have heard.
- *Ask questions for clarification:* seek to clarify before concluding.

- *Avoid asking "why" questions, which often put people on the defensive*: Learn to ask "what" questions instead, "What would cause you to feel that way?" or "What are some of the things that have led you to this place?"
- *Empathize with the other person*: "I can understand why you feel like you do."

Many years ago I worked at a bank. During our training we were taught how to respond to irate customers. One response we were prepared to say is, "I understand why you might be upset. What can we do to resolve it?" That simple statement of identifying with someone went a long way in diffusing the situation.

5. *We must put ourselves in the other person's experience.*

To be a good listener, we have to seek to discover what it is like from the other person's perspective. We need to be willing to enter that person's world and identify with their struggles. That's what Christ did for us. He wanted to relate so badly to each one of us that he humbled himself and entered our world. He asks us to do the same.

> *"The heartfelt counsel of a friend is*
> *as sweet as perfume and incense."*
> *(Proverbs 27:9)*

Listening to another person is a great gift. Some people pay a lot of money to have someone simply listen to him or her. It is the greatest form of acceptance. You don't have to agree or approve of everything that another person says, but listening to another may be the key to greater understanding and deeper relationships.

Talk it Over:

1. In your estimation, "Who is a good listener?" "What makes them so?"

2. What is one principle from this chapter than can help you be a more effective leader?

3. Find someone to help you be accountable to be a better listener this week.

Digging Deeper:

Goulston, M.D., Mark and Keith Ferrazzi. *Just Listen: Discover the Secret to Getting Through to Absolutely Anyone.* New York: AMACOM books, 2010.

Nichols, Michael P. *The Lost Art of Listening: How Learning to Listen Can Improve Relationships.* New York: Guilford Publications, Inc., 2009.

Chapter 9

I Can See Clearly Now

*"The most pathetic person in the world is someone who
has sight but has no vision."*
Helen Keller

A while back I went to the eye doctor to have my eyes
examined. He put a series of letters up on a chart and
said to read them back to him. When I replied, "What letters?"
I knew I was in trouble.

The next several minutes he began putting a series of
lenses before my eyes that brought the letters into clear focus.
Soon my vision was clear and my ability to see in high definition was astounding.

In this chapter we want to look at the subject of vision.
One important skill an effective leader possesses is the ability
to share a captivating vision and be able to communicate
that perspective to others. A leader must be able to invite
and inspire people to join him or her on a journey toward a
destination. As someone shared recently with me, we have to
keep asking the question; What are we trying to do with our
followers? Where are we taking them? How will we know if
we have arrived?

What do we mean by Vision?

"Vision is a clear mental portrait of a preferable future, imparted by God to His chosen servants based on an accurate understanding of God, self, and circumstances."[1]

"Vision is a clear and challenging picture of a ministry as its leadership believes it *can and must be.*" [2]

"Vision is a clear mental picture of what *could be,* fueled by the conviction that it *should be.*" [3]

It's important for leaders to hit the pause button and ask themselves and their team, "What is the goal of what we are trying to do?" As the famous catcher Yogi Berra once said, "When it comes to a fork in the road, take it!" How do we know which road is the correct one to take? How do we communicate the direction God would have us take to those we lead?

The Vision Pathway

A friend of mine once shared this pathway to seeing a vision unfold. It is something I have never forgotten. As you think about the vision that God has implanted in your heart, see if you recognize these steps unfolding.

God first *reveals* the vision to a leader, not to a committee or team.

- The leader *receives* the vision through prayer, contemplation and God's Word.
- The vision is *re-affirmed* by the Word of God
- Other leaders help *refine* the vision.
- The vision is then *relayed* to the people.
- The people *respond* to the vision.
- The vision is then *released* to be implemented by the masses.
- The vision is *reassessed* for its effectiveness.

The Difference Between Mission and Vision

Many leaders confuse mission and vision, particularly when they attempt to communicate it to their followers. The mission of an organization or ministry is open-ended, ongoing, and fairly general in its wording. On the other hand, a vision is specific, measurable, and usually time-bound in its orientation. Let me illustrate it this way: if our mission statement tells us what sport we are playing and puts us inside the stadium, a vision statement tells us how many seats are in the stadium, how many people we want to attract during this season and the next five seasons. It tells us what a win looks like. A vision statement may include portions of our mission statement; it may also help further define what the mission statement functions like in our ministry context.

The Components of a Compelling Vision.

1. *God-* Any vision begins in the heart of God and is given to a leader by God. The vision is unique and has eternal significance. The leader must spend time in the presence of God to hear the heart of God. Jeremiah 29:11-13 says, *"'For I know the plans I have for you,' says the LORD. 'They are plans for good and not for disaster, to give you a future and a hope. In those days when you pray, I will listen. If you look for me wholeheartedly, you will find me.'"*
2. *The ability to envision it-* A captivating vision involves being able to see an ideal future. Warren Wiersbe once said, "A mist in the pulpit causes a fog in the pew." In other words, if you as the leader are confused about the vision, your followers will be even more confused. A great example of a captivating vision is Nehemiah, who had a vision to rebuild the walls around Jerusalem. He envisioned God's people protected to worship God in

safety and security. It required Nehemiah to look through the eyes of faith at the possibilities.

3. *Dissatisfaction-* In order to see a vision enacted, there must be a sense of dissatisfaction with the way things are currently. If I want to lose weight, I first have to become dissatisfied with where I am at before I will do anything to change it. The same is true in ministry.

4. *Timing-* A vision is born in the heart of God, but there must be a readiness by those who are following to see the fulfillment of the vision. A biblical example of this is Joshua, who prepared God's people for a season before he led them into the land God had promised to them. They had waited forty years, and now the time had come to possess the land.

5. *Resistance-* The leader can expect resistance from the inside, the outside, and even above when he or she shares and starts implementing his or her vision. The resistance from within has to do with our fears and our flesh, that fallen part of us that remains even after we give our heart to Christ. You can expect resistance from outside as well, as those who are comfortable do not want to change and don't see the need. There are some who will not buy into the vision no matter how compelling it might be.

Finally, the leader can expect resistance spiritually. The enemy of our faith does not want to see great things happen that bring an advancement of Christ's kingdom. Jesus warned us of this when he said; *"the thief's purpose is to steal and kill and destroy. My purpose is to give them a rich and satisfying life."* John 10:10

6. *Context-* God always gives his vision in a specific context. When God opened the door for Nehemiah to rebuild the walls around Jerusalem, the first thing Nehemiah did was take the time to understand the context. It tells us that

he went out at night to get a look at the ruined walls and their condition before he ever went public with his plans. Every vision is given within a ministry context. Don't try to imitate someone else's vision. First understanding the context of the environment in which you are leading.

7. *Communication-* The leader must be able to communicate the vision in such a way that others see it, catch it and commit to it. Without clearly communicating the vision to the people, the leader may self-sabotage his efforts. Often it requires multiple exposures to the vision before people understand it, appreciate it, and buy into it. It takes even longer for people to commit to it. Someone once told me when you start getting sick of sharing the idea, that is usually the time that your people are just beginning to understand it.

Part of communicating the vision in a compelling way is capturing people's imagination. One way to do that is to use pictures or symbols of a preferable future. Letting people see a glimpse of what could be through imagination is often a way of motivating people towards action.

8. *Goals-* Without benchmarks and goals, we will never know if we are making progress or not. Without goals, we will not know whether to make mid-course corrections. It's hard to measure progress without knowing at what you are aiming.

9. *Perseverance-* A compelling vision must be filled with hope and determination. We hope that God will prevail and provide. There must be a determination to keep at it, through all the ups and downs that may come.

10. *Celebration-* Achieving a compelling vision requires the leader to celebrate progress, not perfection. The leader must choose joy and rejoice along the way. Nehemiah did not just rebuild the walls; he restored the people of

God. God used the walls to unite his people and build their character. When they completed the task, what did they do? They celebrated.

How to Cultivate a Compelling Vision

Get alone with God- Ask God to give you a glimpse of His vision for your ministry. Ask Him to show you what could be and what should be. Ask him to show you areas of your life and ministry where you are dissatisfied.

Talk with your people- listen to what others are saying. Consult with other leaders and seek their input before you go public. You can even send up a trial balloon and see what response you might get.

Ask God to increase your faith- Pray asking God to stretch and grow your faith through this process. If you lack wisdom ask God for it. *"If you need wisdom, ask our generous God and he will give it to you. He will not rebuke you for asking. But when you ask him, be sure your faith is in God alone."* (James 1:5-6)

Seek to confirm the vision through God's Word and prayer- While there may not be a specific chapter and verse to support your vision, there is often a principle that God has revealed in His word that will guide your motives and aspirations.

Go for it.- A friend of mine once said, "The greatest of intentions are nothing compared to the smallest deed done."[4] Too often we talk about the vision rather than acting on it.

After spending time sitting in the chair trying to discern what lens worked best, the optometrist gave me my diagnosis. I have myopia. In other words, I am nearsighted. I have trouble seeing things far away. Maybe you do also. Perhaps the tyranny of the urgent has crowded out any opportunity to dream about the future. It's time to ask God to give us a clear vision of what could be accomplished with the conviction that it must be.

I believe there are still life-changing ministries that need to be started. God is waiting to reveal His vision for His kingdom if we will slow down, listen and allow God's Holy Spirit to show us a glimpse of what could be, followed by a passion and desire to believe and move from what could be to what must be.

Talk it Over:

1. Of the components of a compelling vision mentioned above, which of these is most helpful to you? Which confuses you?

2. If you could do something for God and know you would not fail, what would it be?

3. Take some time this week to ask God to give you a vision of what your life and ministry could look like. Share it with someone this next week.

Digging Deeper:

Barna, George. *The Power of Vision: Discover and Apply God's Plan for Your Life and Ministry*. Ventura: Regal Books, 2003.

Malphurs, Aubrey. *Developing a Vision for Ministry*. Grand Rapids: Baker Books, 2015.

Stanley, Andy. *Visioneering: God's Blueprint for Developing and Maintaining Personal Vision*. Colorado Springs: Multonomah Books, 1999.

Chapter 10

Go S.T.A.R.T. Something!

*"Desire is what motivates us to start,
making a decision is what gets us started,
but discipline is what keeps us going."*
Jim Hanna

As a leader, it is important to know how to be able to both introduce and make positive change. In this chapter we will look at how to take initiative as well as understand how to create a path where organizing and implementing a project will be done successfully.

In order to best understand how to take initiative I would like to use the acronym S.T.A.R.T. Leaders are continually expected to influence and inspire people toward a desired outcome, but how does that happen? Let's take a look.

S= State your goal

The first step is to put in writing and state publicly what your intended goal will be. It is important to be as precise as possible with your goal. I recommend starting with what I have termed "GROW SMART" goals. It is important at the outset of any project to do some pre-planning. You can take a sheet of paper and work through this acronym. G- What is my goal? R-What are the roadblocks and resistance? O- What are my options? W-What will I do about this goal today, this week, this month, this quarter?

Once you have identified the goal, you then move to the SMART portion of project planning. S-Specific: be as specific as possible. M-Measurable: how will you measure this goal? A- Is it Attainable? R-Relevant: How important is this goal? Is it important to you personally? Professionally? Spiritually? Finally, T-Time bound: What is my deadline?

Take a moment and think of a G.R.O.W. S.M.A.R.T. goal and write it here:

Some people don't like the notion of setting goals. Experts tell us that 90% of Americans have no written goals for their lives. If you have some resistance to the word "goals," try changing the terminology, and make them "statements of faith." View them as; areas I want to trust God in my life.

Two things will hinder leaders from taking the initiative. These two predators will keep most people from seeing a goal realized. You need to be aware of them and resist them by praying and pushing through them.

The first is procrastination. Someone has said that procrastination is Latin for the "mess we are in." Procrastination can often come from a variety of sources. Usually, at the heart of procrastination is fear, the fear of failure, the fear we may let others down.

An unknown source wrote this poem about procrastination: "I spent a fortune on an exercise bike and a rowing machine, complete with gadgets to read my pulse and gadgets to prove my progress results. And others to show the miles I charted, but they left off the gadget to get me started."

The second form of procrastination is perfectionism. Many people believe that if they can't do something one hundred percent, they won't do it all. Many have refused to attempt things for God because they have been taught if they don't get it everything completely correct, it's a failure. I call this, "all or nothing" thinking. If it's not all correct, then it's all wrong. There is no in between.

You need to understand that kind of thinking is a lie from the enemy. There is only one perfect person, and that is God. Does God want us to strive for excellence and high quality in what we do? Absolutely! There is a difference, however, between excellence and perfectionism. I once saw a poster that distinguished between the two: "Excellence is doing your best, perfectionism is having to be the best."

I once heard a family counselor say that we need to change our thinking from being "perfect" to being "consistently adequate."[1] She said, " I will never be the perfect parent, spouse, worker, manager or supervisor, but I can strive to be 'consistently adequate.' " I will be the first to admit I have not attained perfection in any of these areas, but my goal today is to be "consistently adequate" in what I do.

The first step is to state your goal. Write it down and think it through. Michael Hyatt says that most people don't even get to the step of having written goals. Taking this step is important but it's not the only thing we need to do.[2]

T- Tear it apart

The next step after setting the goal is to tear it apart. What I mean by this is you have to bombard the goal with several questions. We will get to some of those matters in a moment. This step is where you lay out a timetable of when things need to be done.

You will also need to make a list of what resources you will need to accomplish your goal, and where you will get them. Here are some resources you will need to consider when planning a project:

- What people resources do I need? In other words, "Whom do I need to ask to be involved in this goal?"
- What financial resources are needed? How much is this goal going to cost? What is the budget for this objective?
- How much time will be required? Daily? Weekly? Monthly? Quarterly?
- What physical resources do I need? This has to do with materials, supplies, equipment, etc.
- What other resources do I need? Do I need to consult with someone who has had experience with this objective? Do I need to look at other models of how this is being done already?

The Importance of Reverse Engineering

This term became popular in the computer world but I would like to apply it to the goal or project you planning. Reverse engineering involves choosing your target date for accomplishing your goal. Once you have that date confirmed, you then work backwards. What benchmark dates do you need to create to accomplish your goal?

An example of reverse engineering is the current small group system we use at our church. Three times a year we launch our small groups called Life Groups. Before this date, we have four weekends of promotion. Prior to these promotion dates, there is a catalog that needs to be created listing all of our groups so people can sign up. Before that, there is a planning meeting to discuss the cover design as well as other promotional items. Finally, meetings need to be scheduled to recruit and train new leaders. All of these dates are created with the target launch date in mind.

A- Assign and Act

At this stage, you begin to determine action steps and assign a person's name to those steps. Some of these action items may need to be done by someone else. It is important to discern whether you as the leader need to do these things, or if you should delegate the task.

Michael Hyatt, who has written and spoken on productivity in the workplace, mentions that when it comes to delegation, we need to make clear our expectations. Too frequently, problems enter because the leader was not clear on his or her expectations when delegating. Michael shares five levels of delegation. As a leader you need to clarify what level of delegation you are conferring upon others:

Level 1: Do exactly what I have asked you to do. Don't deviate from my instructions. I have already researched the options and determined what we will do.

Level 2: Research the topic and report back. We will discuss it, and then I, the leader, will make the decision and inform you what I want us to do.

Level 3: Research the topic, outline the options and make a recommendation. Give us the pros and cons of each option, but tell me what you think we should do. If there is agreement with your recommendation, we will move forward.

Level 4: Make a decision and then tell me what you did. I trust you to do the research and make the best decision you can. I only ask that you keep me in the loop. I don't want to be surprised by some unknown information.

Level 5: Make whatever decision you think is best. No need to report back. I trust you completely to make a wise decision. It does not affect the entire team. I know you will follow through. You have my full support.[3]

Also, put a deadline on each assigned task. Without these pieces of a project being assigned a deadline, the puzzle will never come together. Each time you assign a portion of the project, place a deadline upon it.

R- Review Regularly

Your goals must regularly be reviewed in order to monitor progress. If the goals you are working on are urgent, you may need to review them daily. If the goals are more long term in nature you may review them weekly and monthly. I encourage you to *make* time, not *find* the time, to review your goals. If you wait until you find the time, you won't find it. The urgent things will always crowd out the important things. Build it into your schedule. I also encourage you to put your goals in a visible place where you will be reminded of them regularly. If you don't review, you won't pursue your goals.

T- Take Jesus with You

We need to ask God to guide, provide, and be by our side through the whole process. In Proverbs, we read, *"Commit your actions to the LORD and your plans will succeed."* Later Solomon wrote these words, *"we make our plans, but the LORD determines our steps."* (Proverbs 16, 3,9)

We may be able to accomplish some things in this life without God, but when it comes to accomplishing those things that last for eternity, we can only do so through the strength and wisdom that God provides.

Things to keep in mind when implementing what you started

It is important to understand how to create a climate for change so that the outcome will be a positive one. Too frequently leaders have attempted to make changes without considering the factors involved in implementing initiatives.

1. Understand there must be a sense of dissatisfaction for there to be an openness to change. John Maxwell says, "People change when they hurt enough that they have to change, learn enough that they want to change, and receive enough they are able to change."[3] He uses the example that most people will not visit the dentist until they hurt badly enough that they want to see change happen.

    How do you create dissatisfaction? How do you foster a bias for change? One way is to ask questions about the effectiveness of something without providing the answer. As people begin to become aware of the ineffectiveness of something they will be more open to a new initiative.

2. Understand the history of the organization. Realize there is a history with which you are dealing. G.K. Chesterton suggested, "don't take the fence down until you know the reason it was put up."[4]

3. Explain the "why" of change before you answer the "how." In other words explain the purpose of the change. Lead your people to understand the benefits of change for them. As someone once said, "if you get too far out in front of your people you may be mistaken for the enemy."[5]

4. Allow the change to be given a trial period. Ask your followers to consider this new initiative as an experiment. If it doesn't work, we can try something different.

5. Understand the various responses to change. Aubrey Malphurs mentions that when it comes to change, there are four types of people.

    -   *Early adopters-* people in this group are ready to go with the change. These are those who buy in early. On average this group is usually about *twenty* percent.
    -   *Middle adopters-* this group has not made up their mind yet. They need some persuasion. This group is

usually the highest percentage of people. Malphurs says, on average this group is about *fifty-five percent* of the entire group.

- *Late adopters-* this group needs proven results. They are open to the change but they want to see how it benefits them first. This group usually consists of about *fifteen percent* of the group.
- *Never adopters-* no matter what, these people will not change. This group consists of about *ten percent* of people.

When it comes to change, leaders tend to spend a lot of time and energy trying to convince this last group. They try to convince the never adopters. The result is discouragement, defeat and a deflated morale.

The group that the leader needs to spend the majority of his or her time with is the middle adopters. The leader already has the early adopters on board; it is the middle adopters who will create the tipping point for change. If you convince this group, they will influence the late adopters and the change most likely will succeed.

You can see this strategy played out often in a political campaign. Successful candidates don't spend time trying to convince the convinced. They don't worry about the never convinced, realizing they will most likely be unsuccessful in swaying this group. They spend their time and energy attempting to sway the middle adopters.

6. Realize that people need multiple exposures to a proposed change before they understand it and buy in. You have to continually cast the vision. Craig Groeschel said recently, as a leader you are the "CRO, the Chief Reminding Officer."[8] It's the leader's job to remind people constantly of the purpose of what they are doing.

7. Enlist influencers to help bring about the change. These are people who have credibility and can help convince the middle adopters that the change is worth pursuing.

8. Realize that change happens gradually. If a leader makes too many changes too quickly without consulting with his followers, the initiative could easily backfire on him. When followers are not given enough time to process change, they can quickly become paralyzed and non-supportive, either overtly or covertly. Rick Warren says, "people are down on what they are not up on."

9. Have a meeting before the public meeting. In other words take some time to anticipate any resistance you might experience. Having a meeting to prepare will save a lot of misfires when you go public.

10. Realize that the price of leadership is confronting ineffective initiatives.

Max Dupree wrote, "in the end, it is important to remember that we cannot become what we need to be by remaining what we are."[7] Leadership involves evaluating and considering more effective ways of doing things.

As a leader you are expected to be a change agent. As you take some time to reflect on this chapter, I want to encourage you to use the START worksheet and set a goal and see what happens. If the goal impacts others, I encourage you to review and remember the ten principles we have given above.

Talk it Over:

1. What is God impressing upon you to get started?

2. What principles from this chapter have been most helpful?

<u>Digging Deeper:</u>

Malphurs, Aubrey. *Advanced Strategic Planning*. Grand
Rapids: Baker Books, 2013.

G.R.O.W. S.M.A.R.T.
Goals Worksheet

G= Goal: What is my goal? What do I want to accomplish?

_____

R=Roadblocks and Resistance: What are the roadblocks and resistance to reaching this goal?

_____

_____

O= Options: What are my options? List all the possible options available to you.

_____

W=Will: What will I do to reach this goal?
Today: _____
This week: _____
This month: _____
This quarter: _____

S= Specific: Be as specific as possible with your goal.

_____

M= Measurable: How will we measure this goal?

_____

A= Attainable: Is this goal attainable? Why or Why not?

_____

R=Relevant: How important is this goal? Is it important to you personally? Professionally? Spiritually?

_____

_____

T= Time-Bound: What is the deadline for getting this project completed?

Chapter 11

Recruiting People onto Your Team

"Do not hire a man (or woman) who does the work for money; but hire him or her who does it for the love of it."
Henry David Thoreau

Studies have shown that the average church loses between ten to twenty percent of its volunteer workforce each year due to burnout, moving, transferring and unresolved conflict. Others step down because they are facing a personal crisis or challenge of some kind.

If a church does nothing to invite and assimilate new people into ministry positions, it will begin declining and eventually the ministry will no longer be able to sustain itself. A law of physics is the law of entropy. This law says that a system that is closed with nothing added to it, will decline and eventually disappear. The same is true of volunteer organizations.

So how do you recruit new people to be part of your ministry team? If we can understand and practice a few principles when it comes to asking people to serve, we will see new people added to our ministry teams. Let's take a look at some critical things to keep in mind as we seek to recruit, train, motivate and coach volunteers.

Check your Theology on Serving

What you believe to be true about serving will determine the quality and direction that your ministry will take. All of us have a belief about serving. It may be one that says only members can serve, or only the mature can serve. You may have not thought through your theology of serving, but every leader and every church has one.

It is best to start with what the Bible says about servant leadership. While we discussed the meaning of servanthood in chapter four, it is helpful to see this principle reinforced again from the life of Jesus.

The goal of ministry is to help people become like Jesus Christ. We want to see others become like Him in their speech, attitude, thoughts, and actions. We cannot become like Jesus unless we learn to be servants. (John 13:13-17)

The Bible also teaches that every Christ follower has at least one gift to share. (1 Corinthians 12:7, 1 Peter 4:7, 8) Part of discipling other people is helping them discover how God has gifted them, and helping them find places to use those gifts to His glory. We will look deeper into this subject in section three of this book when we look at finding your unique voice and leading from it.

The Bible also teaches that ministry is to be done in teams and not by one person. (Luke 10:1-2) Whenever Paul traveled and established churches, he always journeyed with another person. You will not see ministry done in the New Testament by a lone person.

Finally, the Bible says that we are to be about making and growing new disciples of Jesus. Our task is to show people who come to know Christ that the path to growth and success in the Christian life includes serving others. (Philippians 2: 6-10)

Be Aware of the Barriers to Recruitment

Before we look at what we can do to empower people to serve, it's important to understand why people hesitate to get involved. Without realizing it, the leader may sabotage his or her efforts to add new people to his or her ministry. There are certain obstacles to seeing people recruited and retained. Here are just a few:

- Workers are not sure what is expected of them. They are not given a job description, nor are they coached on what to do.
- Leaders set the wrong tone. They only look to fill slots with warm bodies rather than caring for the person and helping him find the right place to serve.
- Current workers become territorial. They do not share the ministry with others. They see new people as a threat. New people are asking the question when they come to a new church or ministry, "Do I belong?" If they don't sense that they are accepted, they will quickly exit.
- There is unresolved conflict. It's no fun volunteering in a place where there is tension and hurt feelings. People can quickly discern when there is a spirit of competition in a church.
- Volunteers are in the wrong position. In the book "Good to Great," Jim Collins writes about "getting the right people on the bus." Making sure you have the right person in the right position will save you time and energy in the long run.
- Volunteers are given too big of a job with no one to help.
- Volunteers are not given a term limit. They are expected to serve until either they die or Jesus returns.

- Volunteers don't receive any ongoing coaching or encouragement.
- Volunteers are expected to use their personal funds to buy expensive supplies.

Question: Which of the above barriers have you seen in action in your church? Which do you consider the most deadly? Is there one you would add to this list?

Tips for Recruiting

1. *Pray for more workers.* Jesus said these words; *"The harvest is great, but the workers are few. So pray to the Lord who is in charge of the harvest; ask him to send more workers into his fields."* (Luke 10:2) I recently heard a speaker challenge his audience to set an alarm on their phone for every day at 10:02. (You can set smart phones to avoid going off during church services). Every time it goes off, pray Luke 10:2 and ask God to provide the workers needed for your corner of His harvest field.

2. *Understand the power of personal invitation.* The best form of recruitment is to ask personally. It is calling out greatness in someone by affirming them and their potential. I can personally attest to this. The reason I am in a position of church leadership today is because someone saw something in me that I did not see in myself and invited me to serve.

3. *Keep a "hot" list, either mentally or on paper, of people who have the potential to be workers in your ministry.* As you observe or listen to the Holy Spirit, take note of the person God is bringing to mind.

4. *Ask the person to pray about this ministry opportunity for one week.* When I ask someone to serve, I will ask that person to take one week and pray every day about it. I will pray as well and ask God to show him or her if

this serving opportunity is His will for his or her life. It's best not to take longer than a week because people have a tendency to forget. If the person doesn't sense God's leading, it's an indication that it's not a good fit.

5. *Be confident in yourself-* many people struggle with recruitment because they don't believe they can do it. My father, who sold plumbing supplies for thirty-seven years, was so effective as a salesperson; they allowed him to work an additional seven years past retirement age. This is pretty remarkable considering my father never went past the eighth grade in school. He had to quit school before entering high school when his father died, and he went to work to support his mother and nine siblings. He once told me that to be an effective salesperson you have to do three things. First, believe in your product; second, treat everyone as if they are a potential customer; and third, do not promise something to your customers that you are not able to deliver. The same is true as a spiritual leader. You are a salesperson whether you like the terminology or not.

6. *Observe parents when they pick up their children or students.* By looking for parents who interact well with their children, you can often spot those who would be effective volunteers serving in that area. Invite them to pray and consider serving in your ministry.

7. *Have a ministry fair.* Quarterly or semi-annually.

8. *Use seasonal events as recruitment pools, i.e., V.B.S., harvest carnivals and children's Christmas programs.*

9. *Recruit people to a vision and an opportunity, not to a need.* There will always be needs, and what can easily happen is that people get so inundated with needs; they put up a barrier when you ask them to help with a need. Instead, promote it as an opportunity to grow, to love, and to work with some great people.

10. *Practice the "watch one, do one, train one" approach to ministry.* In other words, develop a culture of mentoring in your ministry where seasoned leaders can help mentor new leaders. Give people an opportunity to shadow a seasoned leader and find out about the serving opportunity before they commit full-time to the volunteer position.

11. *Make it FUN!* People gravitate to places where they feel that they belong and can have fun.

12. *Create on-ramps and off-ramps for people.* Give them a clear path to get into ministry, and help them to know there is a gracious way out if it's not a good fit.

13. *Create a welcoming culture.* Let people know that they are welcomed and needed.

14. *Give people the freedom to fail and learn from it.* We are not talking about unrecoverable failures, but in most situations we grow by failing and learning from it. When my kids learned to walk they would take a step and fall down, and then two, three, and more before falling. Pretty soon they were doing more walking than falling. The same is true of new ministry workers.

15. *Affirm new workers through cards, e-mails, texts and small gifts.* Let them know they are appreciated for their service. I strongly encourage you to write a hand written note to your volunteers. I still have notes of appreciation that people have written to me. I'm not sure the reason for it, but a hand written note is more powerful in communicating love and care than an e-mail or formal letter.

16. *Give feedback.* Let them know when they are doing a good job, and help them understand how they can be even more effective.

17. *Celebrate and reward recruitment.* As a ministry leader you need to celebrate what you want to see happen. Here is one prime example. When someone recruits another person onto his team, recognize it and reward it.

18. *Give them opportunities for continuing education and skill sharpening.* It is helpful for volunteers to know that they will have opportunities to grow as a volunteer. Let them know if your system is set up to promote from within, and that there are opportunities to advance in their leadership.

The bottom line is that people want to make a difference with their lives. They want to be part of something bigger than themselves. People will usually resist manipulation and guilt, but will respond to being motivated. The leader must be faithful to make the "ask," or in some cases asking multiple times. It is God who is the One who ultimately motivates a person to serve. When this happens, the results are significant and eternal.

Talk it Over:

1. Which of the above barriers have you seen the most?

2. Which three of the tips given are the most helpful to you?

3. Practice recruiting at least one person to your team and report to someone how it went.

Digging Deeper:

Anderson, Leith and Jill Fox. *The Volunteer Church*. Grand Rapids: Zondervan, 2015.

Morgan, Tony. *Strategic Volunteers*. Loveland: Group Publishing, 2004.

Searcy, Nelson. *Connect: How to Double Your Number of Volunteers*. Grand Rapids: Baker Books, 2012.

Chapter 12

When Leadership
Comes with a Microphone

*"You can have brilliant ideas, but if you can't get them
across, your ideas won't get you anywhere."*
Lee Iaccoca

As part of a young person's requirements to graduate from
seminary, he was expected to speak in chapel to a gath-
ering of his peers. Being deathly afraid of public speaking,
he reluctantly made his way to the platform. In his anxiety,
what he had prepared totally escaped him. He merely asked
a question, "Do you know what I'm going to say?" His peers
shook their head no. He said, "Neither do I! Let's stand for
prayer." After the service was over, his professor approached
him, "Young man, that will not suffice. As a matter of fact,
you will speak again tomorrow in Chapel."

The next day the young man stood at the podium. Once
again, the terror of speaking in front of people set in. He once
again inquired, "Do you know what I'm going to say?" This
time, his peers nodded their head yes. He responded, "Then
there is no sense in me repeating myself. Let's stand for prayer."

When the young man was seated, his superior approached
him even more agitated. "Young man, in order to graduate

from this institution, you will have to speak in front of people and tomorrow you will be expected once again to have something to say."

The third day came, the young man stood at the lectern, and once again he was scared speechless. He once again inquired, "Do you know what I'm going to say?" This time half of his peers shook their head yes and the other half no. He replied, "I'll tell you what, those of you who know, tell those who don't!"

While we will never know if that young man was able to graduate, he left us with a great definition of speaking as a spiritual leader. "Those of you who know, tell those who don't."

Whether you are a public speaker or not, you will be asked from time to time to give a report, share an announcement, give a devotion, teach a class, lead a small group or share your story. What will you say and how will you say it? This chapter is designed to help coach you on how to communicate effectively what God has laid on your heart.

I have put together a set of worksheets that I fill out every time I am asked to speak publicly. While this may seem somewhat academic, it helps me focus my mind and my heart so that God can use me in the way He chooses. Phillip Brooks defined preaching as "truth communicated through your personality."[1] God wants to use your unique personality and His unique story to accomplish unique results.

Begin With Prayer

Every effective sermon, lesson, or spiritual talk starts in the heart of God. If God is the author of His word, doesn't it make sense to consult with the author of the book? Like the creator of a screenplay, God has something in mind for you, but unless you listen to Him through the process, the drama will soon become your own.

One of the worksheets I have created reminds me to pray. I ask myself these questions.

❑ Have I prayed before preparing for the message asking God for His direction and guidance?
❑ Have I prayed while I am preparing the message?
❑ Have I prayed before I speak?
❑ Have I prayed after I speak asking God to use what I have spoken for His purposes?

Ask God to lead you and guide you before you begin preparing. Ask Him to guide your thoughts and ideas. Ask Him to lead you to the passage He wants you to teach. If the passage is already determined, ask God to bring this passage to life as you prepare.

Pray while you are preparing. Pray that God would guide the process of putting this message together, and give you ideas and thoughts that would help explain and apply the text.

Pray before you speak. Since I no longer speak every weekend, I have to pray especially for God's peace and power for the moment. By the time the fourth service occurs at our church, I am experiencing God's peace, but I have to rely even more heavily on His power to make it fresh and relevant. Pray against Satan's activities to discourage you and cause doubt in your mind before you speak. I could write another book on the crazy things that have happened in our home on the night before I have to preach. There have been many times my wife and I have entered into an intense time of prayer for God's deliverance from Satan's harassment of our family on Saturday night.

Pray after you speak. Pray for yourself as you are usually at your lowest emotionally, physically and spiritually after you speak. Pray for the seed that was sown as you spoke, that people would take to heart what God said through His word. Pray that God would help you leave the results of your message with Him. We do not speak in front of people to bring attention and glory to ourselves; we do it so that people will see Jesus and fall in love with Him.

I love what Paul wrote to the church at Corinth about his public speaking. He writes,

"When I first came to you, dear brothers and sisters, I didn't use lofty words and impressive wisdom to tell you God's secret plan. For I decided that while I was with you I would forget about everything except Jesus Christ, the one who was crucified. I came to you in weakness-timid and trembling. And my message and my preaching were plain. Rather than using clever and persuasive speeches, I relied only on the power of the Holy Spirit. I did this so you would trust not in human wisdom but in the power of God." (1 Corinthians 2:1-5)

Sermon in a Sentence/ Sticky Statement

After determining the passage you will speak on, it's time to think through what the passage is saying. Some call this your big idea, others, your sticky statement. What is the one thing that this passage is about, or the *one thing* that you want to emphasize?

This is one of the hardest parts of preparing. It can be time consuming and challenging. But this is where a lot of people who are not trained to speak, do not put in the time. We have all experienced it, haven't we? A person gets up to speak and they don't have a point to their speech. They just ramble on and on, telling one story after another with no continuity, no connection. People walk away saying that was nice or funny or passionate talk, but if you ask them what he or she spoke about, they couldn't tell you.

It has been said that Abraham Lincoln's speaking went straight to the heart because it came from the heart. On the day Lincoln delivered his Gettysburg Address, Edward Everett, who was considered one of the most eloquent orators of that day, preceded him. Everett's speech lasted over two hours. It was a masterful performance. Lincoln, however, sensed the mood of the moment and delivered his entire address in less than two minutes. Everett commented, "I should be glad...if I could flatter myself that I came as near to the central idea of the occasion, in two hours, as you did in two minutes."[2]

What Does the Passage Say?

It's important to take some time to understand what the passage you are speaking about says. It is important to notice the context of the book, the chapter, and the section about which you are teaching. Also, notice key words, such as important words, conjunctions, sentence structure and the tone of the passage. What are the nuances of the passage? Ask yourself if there is any part of this passage that understanding the cultural background would bring additional insight. In their book "Grasping God's Word" authors J.Scott Duvall and J. Daniel Hays state, "Context of a passage determines the meaning of the passage.[3]" You have to understand the context before attempting to speak about the text.

Develop Your Outline

After determining your sermon in a sentence, and taking some time to notice how the passage unfolds, now you can develop your outline. Your main points are meant to support your main idea. Do your main points reflect with the text is saying? Do they help further develop what you want to emphasize? Rick Warren says that to make your main points memorable, put a verb in them. Don't simply outline the passage in a static way, but tell people how the point applies to their life. Some speakers like to make their points parallel, some use alliteration, others prefer neither. There is not one set way to outline a passage. The most important issue is to make it biblical before making it memorable.

Build Your Bridge

Speaking and teaching the Word of God is a lot like building a bridge. David Helm describes this duality in his book "Expository Preaching" You have to start with the "then and there" and move to the "here and now." [4] To do that you have to build a bridge between what the Bible says and how it applies to our lives today. You can do this through stories, illustrations, quotes, and humor. If the outline is the skeleton of your speech or message, then this part of preparation becomes the meat on the bones.

A way to build your bridge from God's Word into the lives of people is to consider two things. First, is to consider your audience, and secondly, your desired outcomes. Let's take a look at some ways you can consider your audience

Consider Your Audience

Another worksheet I fill out as I prepare contains these a set of questions:

What is the challenge to the Non-believer in this sermon?	What is the challenge to the new Christian in this sermon?
What is the challenge to the casual Christian in this sermon?	What is the challenge to the committed Christian in this sermon?

There may be times I don't fill in one of the boxes, but as much as possible I try to include something in my message for each of these four groups. I have found that unless I intentionally think about people in each of these stages of spiritual growth, something will be lacking in my message.

I once heard Bill Hybels share that as he is preparing his message, he pictures several people in his mind. He thinks of people who are in different life situations. As I prepare, here are some of the people I imagine myself addressing.

- What will I say to a person who is angry with God?
- What will I say to the person who is struggling with addiction?
- What will I say to someone who believes that making money is the key to success?
- What will I say to the individual who is walking alone on their journey with Christ?
- What will I say to the young person who is tempted to walk away from God?
- What will I say to the man or woman who has just been diagnosed with cancer?
- What will I say to the single person listening to your message?
- What will I say to the person who is grieving a loss in their life?

I once heard someone say that if you preach to the hurting, you will always have an audience. Your pain and the pain people are carrying with them can be used to demonstrate that the God of hope can fill them with joy and peace, as they trust in Him.

Choose Your Illustrations

The use of illustrations are meant to be windows into your sermon in a sentence. They are not meant to be the main point of your message. These can be stories, illustrations, personal experiences, quotes and fictional citations. Be careful not to find text to fit the illustration. Your illustrations are meant to support your main text, not vice versa.

Consider Your Desired Outcomes

One way to build the bridge into the lives of people is to ask yourself, what am I hoping to accomplish through this message? The following questions have helped me to focus my mind and heart and eventually my message towards these outcomes.

What do I want people to <u>know</u> as a result of this sermon?	What do I want people to <u>feel</u> as a result of this sermon?
What do I want people to <u>do</u> as a result of this sermon?	What do I want people to <u>remember</u> as a result of this sermon?

Finding Your Introduction and Conclusion

Once you have done all of this, you now have a clear sense of what it will take to get into the message, and what it will take to conclude it. I try to use the "hook, look, took" approach. I try to hook people with my introduction, then look at the text, and conclude with practical application. I encourage you to include in your message a clear next step that you want people to take in response to your sermon. It could be giving their life to Christ, recommitting their life to Christ, or taking a clear next step in their faith journey.

Putting It All Together

Now it's time to put all of the pieces of the puzzle together. During this time, I spend time praying and asking God to breathe life into what I am about to do. I usually write one or two drafts of my message before transferring it to my electronic tablet from which I speak. Here are a few things to keep in mind as you write your draft:

- Don't assume people know the Bible. The days of people growing up in the church and having a good working knowledge of the Bible are no longer a reality. If you tell people to turn to a particular text, help them find it.
- Don't jump around from one text to the next. A professor of mine called this "Bible hopscotch." The more passages you turn to, the fewer people track with you. If you want to go outside the passage, refer to it on a screen or put it in your outline.
- If you use a "church" word, explain it. Those who don't know what you mean appreciate it, and those who do know the meaning need the reinforcement.

- Remember, less is more. Leave people wanting to know more, not vice-versa.
- Be careful not to come across angry in your preaching. Learn to smile, laugh. My wife has reminded me on more than one occasion that I look too serious when I preach. Lighten up and enjoy the experience, and everyone else will join you.
- Ask the Holy Spirit to empower you when you speak.
- Keep one finger in the text at all times. In other words, you can share stories and illustrations, but make sure you bring people back to the text.
- Make sure you show them Jesus.

Have a Burden

I first heard this word used when it comes to preaching from Charles Stanley. He says you need to have a burden to share what God has laid on your heart. Again, we probably have experienced both, a person who just speaks because it's the thing to do, and the person who is passionate about what they are sharing.

Have Fun

Speaking should be a delightful experience even for an introvert if you prepared yourself to speak. One thing that has helped me to relax and have fun is something I once heard Rick Warren share, "When you enter the stage and begin speaking, don't ask how do I sound? Or, how am I doing? Instead, ask, what do these people need to hear? What does God want to say through me to this audience that will encourage them to take a step closer to Jesus?"

Here is my challenge to you as a leader. "Those of you who know, tell those who don't!" Do it simply, succinctly, memorably and powerfully. By using the tools that are available, and the power of the Holy Spirit, you can see lives changed and God's Word take hold in a people's lives.

Talk it Over:

1. What part of this chapter is the most helpful to you?

2. Which part of this chapter is the most challenging?

3. What is one thing you can begin using as you prepare to speak?

Digging Deeper:

Helm, David R. *Expository Preaching: How we Speak God's Word Today.* Wheaton: Crossway, 2014.

Maxwell, John C. *Everyone Communicates but Few Connect: What the Most Effective People do Differently.* Nashville: Thomas Nelson, 2010.

Robinson, Haddon. *Biblical Preaching.* Grand Rapids: Baker Publishing Group, 2014.

Chapter 13

Time Keeps on Slipping

"Most plans fail because of lack of focus, not a lack of time; we all have the same amount of time."
Author Unknown

"I magine there is a bank that credits your account each morning with $86,400 pennies. It carries no balance from day-to-day, and every evening it erases whatever part of the balance you failed to use during the day. What would you do? Draw out every cent, of course!

"Each of us has such a bank. Its name is 'time.' Every morning God credits you with 86,400 seconds and every night it writes off as lost whatever portion of this you have failed to invest to good purpose. It carries no balance; it allows no overdrafts. Each day it opens a new account for you. There is no going back, no drawing against 'tomorrow.' You must live in the present on today's deposits. The clock is running; make the most of today."[1]

What do you and I, your boss, your pastor, the Mayor of your city and the President of the United States, all have in common? We all have the same amount of time in a day to get things done. No matter what education we may have had or not had, we cannot add an extra hour or two to our day. (Unless it's daylight savings time or leap year!)

Years ago, I heard a message by Rick Warren that changed how I approach my time. I have never forgotten his outline. It will form many of the thoughts for this chapter. While I have added some things along the way, I realize I can't compete with Rick's memorable outline, based on the following Scripture:

The Apostle Paul wrote these words:

"So, be careful how you live. Don't live like fools, but like those who are wise. [16] Make the most of every opportunity in these evil days. [17] Don't act thoughtlessly, but understand what the Lord wants you to do. [18] Don't be drunk with wine, because that will ruin your life. Instead, be filled with the Holy Spirit, [19] singing psalms and hymns and spiritual songs among yourselves, and making music to the Lord in your hearts. [20] And give thanks for everything to God the Father in the name of our Lord Jesus Christ." (Ephesians 5:15-18)

Analyze Your Activities

The first thing we need to do is begin with a time audit. Paul says. *"So, be careful how you live."* Paul uses the word "blepo" which means take a "close look at or examine closely." Managing our time as leaders begins by pausing to reflect on how we are using our time. Simple questions to ask are: "Am I satisfied with the use of my time right now?" "Am I getting those things assigned to me done in a timely manner?" "Do I have time to plan ahead or am I driven by the next project and its deadline?" If you are like me, there is an abiding sense that I could manage my time better.

Today there are a lot of time wasters that will rob us of our time if we are not careful. Here are just a few time bandits:

- *Social Media-* We can spend countless hours looking at insignificant material.
- *E-mail-* The electronic bandit called e-mail can steal our time if we are not careful. We can spend a large amount of time responding to insignificant messages.
- *Phone apps-* Let's face it, phone apps are great, but they can also be a time bandit.
- *Netflix-*™ It is possible in this day and age to know more about the character in the series that we are watching than the person of Christ.
- *Video Games-* We can spend an inordinate amount of time trying to get to the next level or gain victory over our competition. We now have the capacity to compete against people from all over the world. We no longer have to wait to play a game against a friend or relative.
- *Previously recorded television shows and movies.* There is a new stressor nowadays called "stacking." This angst occurs when too many of your recorded shows stack up and you can't watch all of them.
- *Drop ins-* people who aren't using their time wisely and want to waste your time as well.

Learning to use our time wisely begins by taking a close look at where our time is going and how can we prevent time wasters. We have to be intentional with our use of time. If you don't have a plan for how you use your time, everyone else will.

Categorize Your Schedule

Paul uses two categories, *"wise and unwise."* A question that a leader must continually ask, "Is this the best use of my time right now?" With all the distractions that come at us, it is easy to let our schedule slip into the unwise category rather than the wise.

Steven R. Covey shares a time matrix in which he divides time into two categories, "urgent" and "important." Below is his time quadrant.

	Urgent	**Not Urgent**
Important	**I** - Crisis - Pressing Issues - Deadlines - Meetings	**II** - Preparation - Planning - Prevention - Relationship building - Personal Development
Not Important	**III** - Interruptions - Some mail - Many popular activities	**IV** - Trivia - Some phone calls - Excessive TV/Games - Time wasters

The upper left quadrant consists of those things that we have to do. They are both "important" and "urgent." They include deadlines, pending projects, essential communication with people, etc.

The lower left quadrant consists of those things that are "urgent" but not "important." These are things that appear to be "important" but are not. They can eat up our time if we are not careful. These are often things that can be passed along to have someone else do.

The upper right is the "important" but not "urgent" things. These are things are not life or death at the moment, but are "important" to our well-being. There are things such as a quiet time with God, physical exercise, personal enrichment, relationship building. If we are not careful, this is where we steal time. We will sacrifice the things that are "not urgent" but "important" for the other three quadrants. In doing so, we are setting ourselves up for burnout and health problems down the road.

The lower right quadrant contains those things that are "not important" and "not urgent." They are those mindless, meaningless activities that will slowly and secretly invade our lives leaving us unproductive and unfulfilled. They include things such as watching television, movies, social media, etc.

If we are going to find more time in our schedule, we have to take it from the bottom two quadrants. Our livelihood depends on the upper left quadrant and our personal well-being depends on the upper right. That being the case, we cannot take from these two. What's left is to take it from the "urgent" but "not important" and the "not important", "not urgent" zones. But how do we do that? Covey goes on to further explain his matrix.

URGENCY

High   Low

	1	**2**
IMPORTANCE (High)	Urgent **and** important Do it now	Important **not** urgent Decide when to do it
	4	**3**
(Low)	Urgent **not** important Delegate it	**Not** important **not** urgent Dump it

Those things that are "urgent" and "important" we need to be done now. Those things that are "important" but "not urgent," we have to block time and space for them. The things that you consider "urgent" but "not important" can be delegated to someone else. Finally, those things that are "not

137

important" and "not urgent" we need to consider eliminating or reducing.

Prioritize Your Opportunities

Paul goes on to say, *"making the most of every opportunity in these evil days."* I'm not sure who said it first, but it applies here, "those who fail to plan, plan to fail." Paul tells us we need to maximize our time because the days are evil. Some translations of this verse say we are to "redeem the time," which means we are to intentionally buy back the time that would otherwise be used for evil. If we don't prioritize our schedules, the urgent things will always win.

How Do I Prioritize My Schedule?

1. *Make a to do list.* Each day before I go home from work, I make a to do list for the next day. When I come into the office in the morning, I review and evaluate it.

   The problem with a to do list is that the items on the list vary widely in value. If we only have a to do list and don't prioritize it, the most important things may not get done.

2. *Give each item on your to do list a number or letter from most important to least.* Start with the most important and work your way down. That way, if you don't get everything done on your list, you have at least accomplished the most important.

3. *Make a decision*

   • Do it now- those things that are urgent/important.
   • Decide when you will do it- those things that are not urgent/important.

- Do it through others- those things that are urgent/ not important.
- Don't do it- learn to use your no muscle with the things that are not "important" and not "urgent."

4. *Delegate the task*

Many leaders have difficulty delegating a task. Sometimes pride can get in the way and we tell ourselves that no one can do it quite as good as we can, so we just do it ourselves. Let's face it, one of the reasons we attained the position we have is because we did our job well and others affirmed us. The problem is, without equipping and training others, the leader becomes the bottleneck to growth and effectiveness.

Another reason we fail at delegation is because we don't clearly communicate what we expect when we delegate. One leadership axiom I try to live by is this, "no one I work with ever complained that I communicated too much." It is when I under-state the responsibilities and expectations involved that I get myself in trouble.

A reason that delegation often fails is we don't *inspect* what we *expect* from people. We fail to ask the questions of progress and challenge along the way. We neglect to ask, "How are we doing with this?" "Is there anything you need from me to help you accomplish this task? "When can I expect to have a report or the results?"

Also, we disregard asking, "What challenges are you facing with this project?" "Is there anything you don't understand about what you are being asked to do?" These are important questions to ask if delegation is going to be successful.

Utilize the Present

Paul writes, *"Make the most of every opportunity in these evil days."* The greatest enemies of productivity today are guilt, worry, and procrastination. Guilt robs us of the energy to focus on today. We are remorseful of things that have happened. We live in regret of things we cannot change but from which we can learn. We need to ask God's help in letting go of the past and maximizing the present. Guilt can cripple our productivity.

The other enemy is worry. Worry keeps us so focused on the future and what might happen it keeps us from focusing on today and what God has called us to do today. We need to live in the present, not in the "if only's" and "what if's." We need to replace these " what if's" and "if only's" with "God is." God is able to give us the grace we need to accomplish what He asks us to do.

A final time bandit is procrastination. The dictionary defines procrastination as "the act or habit of putting off or delaying, especially something requiring immediate attention."[3] One of the greatest causes of procrastination is fear. We fear getting into the task and not having enough time to complete it. The task looks overwhelming to us. The key is doing something even if we don't complete it. In order to do this we have to deny how we feel about the task and will ourselves to do it at first.

The risky reality is that the "urgent" things crowd out the "important" things, and we resign ourselves to saying we just don't have time to attend to that project. That's why prioritizing your to do list is important. It helps us recognize those that not everything on your to do list carries the same value. Some things are more important than others.

Recognize What's Most Important

Paul gives these instructions to be productive, *"Don't act thoughtlessly but understand what the Lord wants you to do."* Are you taking the time to understand what God's unique will is your life? Are you taking the time to discover His agenda for your day? Through prayer, Bible intake, and godly people, are you taking the time to understand the plans God has you?

It's easy to sacrifice what's most important at the altar of the urgent. We have to be intentional about listening and discovering God's will our lives.

Equalize the Pressure

Paul tells us that we need *"to be filled with the Holy Spirit."* The word "filling" means to be controlled by the Holy Spirit. It was used of wind filling the sail of a ship and empowering the ship to move. This word is also in the present continuous tense, in other words, it literally says, *"keep being filled with the Holy Spirit."*

How do I become filled with the Holy Spirit? By surrendering control of my life to God and confessing any known sin that stands between God and me. We give God the center seat at the table of our lives. Have you ever seen the President of the United States when he meets with his cabinet? He is always in the center chair. God doesn't just want to be resident in your life; he wants to be President.

How do we know when someone is filled with the Holy Spirit? He or she will demonstrate the fruit of the Holy Spirit. Paul says elsewhere, *"But the Holy Spirit produces this kind of fruit in our lives: love, joy, peace, patience, kindness, goodness, faithfulness, gentleness, and self-control."* (Galatians 5:22)

Can we lose the control of the Holy Spirit? Yes, by willfully and knowingly sinning. When we do that, we "grieve the Holy Spirit." (1Thessalonians 5:19.) The way we are controlled once again by the Holy Spirit is by confessing our sin and surrendering to God.

The one thing about time is that we will never be given more as we go along. We need to manage and redeem the time that God has given to us. I encourage you to look back on this chapter and find one thing that you can begin practicing right now that will help you take full advantage of the time He has given you.

Exercise: Make a matrix like the one given in this chapter and put the activities in your life in each quadrant. After categorizing your activities, determine whether you need to eliminate or adjust your time to provide more time to do what's most important.

Why not ask God to help you take a close, honest look at how you use your time? If Christ is Lord of our lives, doesn't it make sense he would be Lord of our time as well?

Talk it Over:

1. What do you need to start doing today to manage your time more wisely?

2. What do you need to stop doing to manage your time more wisely?

Digging Deeper:

Allen, David. *Getting Things Done: The Art of Stress Free Productivity.* New York: Penguin Books, 2001.
Pressfield, Steven and Seth Godin. *Do the Work: Overcome Resistance and Get Out of Your Own Way.* Do You Zoom, Inc, 2011.

Chapter 14

Giving Spiritual Counsel Without Being the Counselor

"A leader is one who knows the way,
goes the way and shows the way."
John Maxwell

As a spiritual leader, you will be asked by others to give spiritual counsel. In most cases, people consult with a friend or someone they know when they have a crisis before turning to a paid professional. What will you say when someone begins to share their heart with you?

The Case for Giving Spiritual Counsel

Throughout the Scriptures there is support for giving spiritual guidance. The prophet Isaiah spoke about the coming Messiah. While these words are true of Jesus, they are also characteristic of the person who follows Christ.

"The Spirit of the Sovereign LORD is upon me,
for the LORD has appointed me to bring
good news to the poor.

143

He has sent me to comfort the brokenhearted
And to proclaim that captives will be released
and prisoners will be freed...
To all who mourn in Israel, he will give a
crown of beauty for ashes,
A joyous blessing instead of mourning,
festive praise instead of despair.
In their righteousness, they will be like great oaks that the
LORD has planted for his own glory."
(Isaiah 61:1,3)

In the New Testament, Paul wrote; *"Share each other's bur-dens, and in this way obey the law of Christ"*(Galatians 6:1) What is the law of Christ? Jesus said clearly that the law could be summed up in these words, *"Love the Lord your God with all your heart, soul, mind and strength and love your neighbor as yourself."* (*(Matthew 22:37-39)* The way to "obey the law of Christ" is by loving your neighbor as yourself.

Finally, James, in his letter to suffering friends instructed them, *"Confess your sins to each other and pray for each other so that you may be healed."* (James 5:16)

These verses make it clear that every Christ follower is called to be available as a spiritual support for others with whom we come in contact. I believe that the Bible teaches the "priesthood of all believers," which means that every Christian is a representative of Jesus Christ and can provide care for people not just paid professionals.

A Plan to Counsel Others

When I counsel with someone, there is a track that runs through my mind as I listen to the person share. I usually have the letters I.G.O.U running through my mind. Let me unpack this for you.

I- What are the Issues?

I first begin by either asking or helping the person identify what issues are causing them stress. Heather Zempel in her book "Community is Messy," identifies three messes that people often are struggling with; they are "sin messes, relational messes and life messes."[1] I would add another, "identity messes." Larry Crabb has written that the two greatest needs in a person's life are significance and security. [1] It is our role as a people helper to guide them in discovering that both of these needs are ultimately found in Jesus Christ.

G- What Does God Think About This?

It is important to direct the person to what God thinks about their situation. I recently read Paul's words in 2 Corinthians 10 as he describes what ministry entails, *"We are human, but we don't wage war as humans do. We use God's mighty weapons, not worldly weapons, to knock down the strongholds of human reasoning and to destroy false arguments. We destroy every proud obstacle that keeps people from knowing God. We capture their rebellious thoughts and teach them to obey Christ."* (2 Corinthians 10:3-5)

The last phrase struck me, how much of ministry is about correcting people's faulty thinking? How much of ministry is helping people capture their rebellious thoughts and teach them to obey Christ? We do that by helping them discover the truth of what God says in His Word. Jesus said, *"You will know the truth, and the truth will set you free."* (John 8:32) It is important to be in the Word for ourselves as leaders so we can help direct people who need a Word from God.

O- What are Your Options?

Part of counseling is helping people to identify their options concerning their issue. What biblical options does the person have? Giving counsel is helping people to see that there is a better way. Helping people discover that there are other prudent options than what they are struggling with is an important goal of counseling.

U- What Will You do About This?

Helping people determine their next step is also a part of giving spiritual counseling. It is important to remember that as a counselor it is ultimately their choice whether to follow your counsel or not. You cannot force people to follow your instructions. They have to choose for themselves.

Things to Avoid When Giving Spiritual Counseling

When called upon to counsel another, here are some things to keep in mind. These are things I have done and learned the hard way they don't work.

1. *Avoid talking too much.* Our greatest asset as a counselor is to be a good listener. When Job experienced great loss and suffering, his three friends showed up. Before they began assuming why Job was ill, they sat for seven days and didn't say anything to Job. (Job 2:13) I call this the ministry of presence. Having someone present and willing to listen is something people are craving these days.

2. *Avoid being judgmental.* There will most likely come a time in your counseling when you will need to speak truth to the person, but avoid being judgmental.

Sidestep statements like "How could you do such a thing?" or "Why did you do that?"

There is a difference between acceptance and approval of someone. Acceptance says I love you because Jesus loves you, but I do not agree with your behavior or decision. It's important to accept the person you are counseling without having to approve of their choices.

3. *Avoid pious platitudes.* The longer we have been Christians, the easier it is to slip in the lofty language that we think will help someone but it may create more despair than repair. In a recent article, Joe McKeever wrote: "21 Things not to say to a Hurting Friend."[2] Here are the top ten in my estimation.

"Here's why I think God did this."

- "If you had enough faith, your problems would be solved."
- "God works all things together for good."
- "You must feel good about where your loved one is now; they cannot suffer any more."
- "Lots of people have gone through this."
- "It's been a long time; you really need to get over this and move on."
- "I know how you feel, I know what you are going through."
- "It's the Lord's will you know."
- "Just pray about it and everything will be fine."
- "That's nothing, let me tell you about my woes."

4. *Avoid assuming you know the person's problem.* Some people immediately jump to using the sin lens, and see the other person's problem as a result of some sin in his or her life. They will jump to challenging the person to repent, without realizing that it's the Lord's kindness (and

yours) that leads to repentance. (Romans 2:4) Also, people may assume they know the person's problem because they have had a similar experience. "I know exactly how you feel," is not only inappropriate, it's inaccurate. Stay curious, my friend!

5. *Avoid taking the place of the Holy Spirit.* Stay clear of saying "This is what I would do if I were you..." We are not that person, and we are not the Holy Spirit. We need to leave room for the Holy Spirit to convince of sin, righteousness and judgment. That's not our role.

6. *Avoid taking responsibility for the other person's problems.* This may be difficult for those of us who are very caring people. We want to make things better for other person and relieve the hurt, but sometimes pain is an indicator that something deeper is going on. Don't short change the process by bailing the person out. The Apostle Paul wrote, *"Each person must carry his own load."* (Galatians 6:5)

7. *Avoid giving simple solutions to complex problems.* It's not wrong to recommend Bible verses, a book, a sermon or other resources, but be careful not to assume that the problems will just go away if that person reads or hears a particular resource.

Some Things to Keep in Mind When Counseling Someone

1. *Gently help the person discover what the issues are and what they are going to do about them.* Our role is not to be the judge, jury and prosecuting attorney in that person's life.

2. *Help a person label their emotions.* Often people aren't sure what they feel. Helping them identify their emotions is the first step in helping them learn how to deal with them. To do this, when counseling a man or husband,

I start with "What do you think about this?" or "What are you thinking right now?" I have found that under a man's thoughts are some deep feelings, but it's a process to get there.

When counseling a wife, I ask, "How do you feel about this?" or "What are you feeling right now?" I have found that the starting place for a female is most often talking about her feelings. Underneath those feelings are some deep thoughts, but we have to dig past the emotions to get to them.

3. *Understand that underneath every emotion and thought is a belief fueling those feelings and thoughts.* Helping people change their belief system about God, about themselves and others is the both the challenge and goal of counseling. Replacing false beliefs with the truth is a major objective in counseling.

4. *Speak the truth in love.* Both of these are important. Someone has said that love without truth is a fantasy, but truth without love is brutality. Both are important to have healthy relationships. When the time comes to speak truth to a person, we must do so in love, recognizing that God loves this person and is asking us to love him or her enough to be honest with him or her.

5. *Work at creating a safe place and being a safe person.* Being a "safe" person means we need to be a confidential person. It's important not to repeat the person's problems unless he or she gives us permission to do so, or unless we make a disclaimer that we will share this with our spouse or our pastor. I learned this the hard way. A few years back I counseled a husband who was having an affair. He shared with me that he had a series of e-mails he wrote and wanted me to look them over. He told me at that time, that he had shown these messages to his wife. He collected a set of e-mails he kept every time they had

an argument. He maintained a record of the issues and causes of their conflict.

A few days later I received a phone call from the wife, asking me if her husband had said anything about having a book of e-mails he was going to send out to people. I told her he had shown me some e-mails and told me that she was already aware of them. Unbeknownst to me, her husband listened on another line she had conferenced him in on. When I shared that piece of information, he quickly interrupted and erupted into a tirade of how could I share this and consider myself a pastor. As much as I tried to explain myself, he would not listen and eventually hung up on me. Needless to say that couple's marriage did not survive and neither stayed in our church. Ouch!

I will say that it is important to keep things confidential, but if someone is threatening to hurt himself or herself or another person, you are required by law in many states to contact the authorities. In cases of suspected sexual abuse, you are required as well.

6. *Realize that we have a great resource, the Holy Spirit who is called the Counselor.* (John 14:26) The Holy Spirit will guide us and help us with what to say in a given situation. We must listen to His promptings as we counsel the other person.
7. *Don't underestimate the power of praying for the other person.* I try to close every counseling session with prayer. I appeal to the Holy Spirit, who lives inside the person I'm counseling to reveal to him or her what the next right step is in his or her life. I ask God to comfort that person, provide for him or her and relieve the pain and pressure he or she is facing.

The Plan of Salvation

One thing that is important to have in our toolbox is a tool for leading someone to faith in Jesus Christ. The greatest need a person has is to have a personal relationship with his or her Creator through the person of Jesus Christ. As spiritual leaders, there will be opportunities for us to share God's plan for life.

Personally, there are two simple methods I use when sharing Christ. There may be more elaborate methods, but I want to give you something you can remember and use. First, is what I call my "elevator approach." If I only have the same amount of time as an elevator ride, what would I say?

I simply tell them that the difference between biblical Christianity and all the other world religions is the difference between "*do* versus *done.*" All the other religions of the world and even some Christian religions say we have to do good deeds to have the possibility to make it into heaven. I have been a good person, try real hard, do penance, keep the five pillars of the faith, go door to door, and if I am ardent and zealous, then God is obligated to accept me.

Biblical Christianity says: It's done! The price has been paid in full! It is finished! I can't do enough good things to gain favor with God. It's been done for me. Christ did what I could not do for myself when He died in my place. He gave his life for me so that I could have life in and through Him. (2 Corinthians 5:21) Christ offers salvation as a gift that is *"by grace through faith, it is not by works so that no one can take credit for it."* (Ephesians 2:8,9)

The second method explains the difference between religion and a relationship with Christ. Religion is man's attempt to reach up to God, to be good enough. The type of relationship that God wants us to have is God reaching down to us. God reached down to us in our sin and brokenness and

151

revealed himself to us. He simply asked us to say yes to Him and his offer of forgiveness and hope.

In using either of these approaches, I often include my own story. Everyone, no matter how long they have been a believer, has a story to share. I once was like this, and now Christ is living in me and changing my life. Your story intersecting with His story is a hard for a non-believer to refute.

There have been many times when God has opened a door for me to share His love offering through Jesus Christ with someone who came to me for counseling. In the midst of the pain, Christ can offer that individual peace, hope, and joy. Most of all, He desires to give to them the greatest Counselor the world has ever known.

Being a leader means being a people-helper. Inevitably we will be asked to give someone advice and counsel as we guide him or her toward their goal. What we say and how we say it can have a profound impact on the direction a person takes with his or her life.

A few years back I was hired to be a chaplain for a business in the town where I lived. Twice a week I made an on-site visit. I sat in the lunchroom and made myself available to anyone who wanted to talk. I then walked around and casually visited with people and asked them how it was going. No one was eager to open up. Most of them thought I worked for management and was sent to spy on them. But then over time, a lady lost her husband to cancer. I was able to talk with her, counsel her, give her some literature, pray for her and keep in touch with her. Due to my interactions with her, others began to talk to me about stresses in their family and marriage. This breakthrough happened simply because I took the time to listen to one person who experienced loss.

As leaders, we will have moments like this as well, when people will look to us for help. We must not shy away from these opportunities, as they may be thing that people remember about our leadership the most.

Talk it Over:

1. Which principle given in this chapter has been the most helpful to you?

2. Have you found as a leader that people are willing to seek you out for advice? Why? Why not?

Digging Deeper:

Clinton, Timothy, Dr. Archibald Hart, George Ohlschager. *Caring for People God's Way*. Nashville: Thomas Nelson, 2009.

Collins, Gary. *How to be a People Helper*. Ventura: Vision House/Regal, 1995.

Crabb, Larry. *Effective Biblical Counseling*. Grand Rapids: Zondervan, 2007.

Chapter 15

Dealing with Conflict as a Leader

"Where there's light, there's bugs."
Chuck Swindoll

I still remember a friend telling us a story in a class when I was in College about how his church split over a chicken wing. Apparently, there were some in leadership who believed a certain way theologically, and would not allow room for any disagreements. The situation went way beyond that of a doctrinal dispute to a point where the two sides moved to building a case against one another and believing that the other side was living in sin. At the annual church picnic, one leader led in prayer. He thought he would begin by proving his point. He began by raising the chicken wing up and proclaiming, "On this day in history it has been predestined that I eat this chicken wing!" A dissenter who was standing near this man, retorted, "No It's not," and grabbed the chicken wing out of the man's hand and began eating it! The result of the melee was a church split.

While most of us have not experienced conflict to this level, we have seen disagreements develop into an all out war. As leaders, we will inevitably encounter conflict. Someone once said, "With any change, there is conflict." It is crucial to learn how to respond and resolve those skirmishes when they happen. In this chapter we want to share some tools that can help when clashes occur.

What is Conflict?

The word conflict comes from a Middle English word and means, "to strike together." When there are two or more people placed into an environment of living and working together, there will inevitably be a difference in values, desires and needs.

Here is how I define conflict: "Conflict happens when there is a difference with another person or group in perception, preferences, passions, priorities and practices." Let's dissect this definition and see what we can learn.

First, conflict can happen when we have a difference in *perception*. Those who are married know that it doesn't take long to realize that husbands and wives see things from different perspectives. That doesn't necessarily make one perspective right and the other wrong, just different. As one author writes, "men hear things through blue hearing aids, women through pink."[1] Sometimes this can cause conflict. Often conflict is caused by misunderstanding or misinterpreting what another person said or did.

Secondly, conflict can happen when *preferences* collide. Our preferences have to do with our what we are used to doing. Preferences are those things that we have done in the past and have found enjoyment in doing them; they have become important to us. These things that may not necessarily be black and white, but can become to us. Unfortunately, there is no book in the Bible called "opinions." We form our opinions based on what is important to us. Sometimes our preferences are formed by the way we were raised. Certain traditions and ways of doing things can become divisive if others do no see the same importance.. The downside is that our preferences can prevent us from hearing and understanding the other person.

A third collision that causes conflict is a difference in our *passions*. Our passions are those desires that are both good and bad. The reality is we still have to deal with the fallen part of our spiritual lives, if we don't, conflict arises. The Apostle James put it this way,

> *"What is causing the quarrels and fights among you? Don't they come from the evil desires at war within you? You want what you don't have, so you scheme and kill to get it. You are jealous of what others have, but you can't get it, so you fight and wage war to take it away from them. Yet you don't have what you want because you don't ask God for it. And even when you ask, you don't get it because your motives are all wrong- you want only what will give you pleasure."* (James 4:1-3)

James tells us that there are three causes of conflict. One is competing desires. When two people both want something they are not getting, there is conflict.

A second reason for conflict is selfish ambitions. When our desires become fueled by selfishness and thinking only of my needs, conflict easily gets out of control. James says; *'You want what you don't have, so you scheme and kill to get it."*

A final reason that we experience conflict is because of self-reliant attempts to resolve conflict. Again James writes, *"Yet you don't have what you want because you don't ask God for it."* When we are in conflict our natural tendency is to default to either avoid the conflict or to attack each other by becoming defensive and deflecting what is being said to us.

Relationships get messy when our sinful side rises up and leads the charge in the midst of the conflict. We can become defensive, critical, and feel that we need to prove ourselves right rather than repair the relationship.

Not all passions are wrong. When we become passionate about a certain area that is biblical and right, it motivates us to action. Our desires cause conflict however, when we do not understand why others are not as passionate as we are about something. We can become angry and frustrated, and allow it to build a wall between others and us.

Our *priorities* can be a major source of conflict. These have to do with our values, those things we hold important. When we perceive that our core values are violated, sparks often fly. The challenge of conflict is to hold these things as important but at the same time seek to understand the other person and what is valuable to them.

Finally, the last leadership landmine to navigate through is differences in *practices*. When others do things we don't agree with or understand, it can cause problems. We may determine that their actions are inappropriate, selfish or sinful. When we come to that conclusion, conflict commences.

How to Navigate Leadership Landmines

The good news in all of this is that Jesus did not leave His spiritual leaders to try to navigate through this obstacle course on their own. There are some practical and helpful principles found in God's Word that can guide us through this potentially disastrous process.

In Matthew 18, Jesus gave us a process to follow that can help us resolve conflict as leaders. While these steps do not a guarantee a positive outcome, they can help us increase the likelihood that the conflict will be dealt with in a healthy, constructive way.

Jesus said these words

*"If another believer sins against you, go pri-
vately and point out the offense. If the other
person listens and confesses it, you have won
that person back. But if you are unsuccessful,
take one or two others with you and go back
again, so that everything you say may be
confirmed by two or three witnesses. If the
person still refuses to listen, take your case
to the church. Then if he or she won't accept
the church's decision, treat that person as a
pagan or a corrupt tax collector. I tell you
the truth, whatever you forbid on earth will
be forbidden in heaven, and whatever you
permit on earth will be permitted in heaven."*
(Matthew 18:15-18)

Much of the following section first came as result of listening to a sermon series by James MacDonald called "Always
Resolve Everything Now: The Key to Lasting Relationships."
In this series, Dr. MacDonald gives a step-by-step process
based on Matthew 18. I have taken these steps and added
some insights from my experience. Let's take a look.

How to Resolve Conflict

1. *Make sure it's a big deal.* Jesus said, *"if your brother or
   sister sins."* It's important to do a little inventory before
   addressing the issue, and make sure it's not a personal
   preference that is causing the conflict.

   If it's not a big deal, we can forget about it. As the song
in Frozen says, "let it go." There are many times as leaders
we will need to "let it go." Ruth Graham said, "Marriage is
the union of two great forgivers." The same is true in leadership relationships.

We can *pray about it*. We can talk to God about it, asking Him to help us let it go. We can also ask Him for wisdom in how to deal with the issue. We also need to ask God to "search our heart" and reveal any wrong motives for feeling the way we do. If we have attempted to forget about it and have prayed about it, and it is still troubling us, then we take the next step.

2. *Take the Initiative*. The next step is to go and seek clarification. You don't go with your mind made up. (Jumping to conclusions is a favorite indoor sport for many leaders.) You go to the other person humbly, prayerfully, seeking to understand why they did or said that thing that offended you. James, the brother of Jesus, says, *"You must all be quick to listen, slow to speak, and slow to get angry. Human anger does not produce the righteousness God desires."* (James 1:19-20)

If the offense is still troubling us, we need to go and talk to the person. Don't go with a judgmental spirit, instead go seeking to understand and restore the relationship. The Apostle Paul gave us this warning. *"Dear brothers and sisters, if another believer is overcome by some sin, you who are godly, should gently and humbly help that person back onto the right path. And be careful not to fall into the same temptation yourself."* (Galatians 6:1)

What I am about to share with you is worth the price of this book. It is something that I have learned in recent years that has revolutionized how I approach a conflict. When I am led to take action, *I stay at a place of uncertainty until I get clarity on the issue*. In other words, don't assume or jump to conclusions about what has happened. Approach the matter with a spirit of humility that is demonstrated by telling yourself that you may not have all the facts, or I misunderstood, or maybe my perception is wrong.

The question is often asked, "When do I know I need to go and address the issue?" In other words, when should I confront someone and when should I let it go?

Ken Sande has some helpful insights regarding this matter. "I need to go when a conflict damages my relationship with someone." "I need to go when a conflict is hurting others." "I need to go when a conflict is hurting the offender." "I need to go when a conflict is significantly dishonoring God." [2]

3. *Go privately at first.* This step may be one of the hardest parts of dealing with confrontation. Having the courage to go and sit down with someone can appear to be overwhelming. I think some of our fear is due to some of the lies the enemy of our faith tells us. One such lie is, things won't get better; they will get worse instead of better. There is a relational risk we take by being obedient to God, but the result is internally we have a clear conscience in knowing we did the right thing and attempted to resolve the matter.

Another such fear we struggle with is that the person may not acknowledge he or she did anything wrong, or may blame us for the offense. While these fears may paralyze us and prevent us from addressing the issue, it's important to know that when we are attempting to do what God asks, He promises to be present in a powerful way. (1 Corinthians 5:4)

When we go and have a crucial conversation with someone about how he or she might have offended us, it's important to keep the following guidelines in mind:

- Avoid statements of motive.
- Believe the best in the other person. Give grace when he or she has failed.

- Confront the behavior or the action, not the person- It is best to say, "When you did or said this, I felt
  _____."

- Using "I" statements helps us avoid making accusations.

4. *Be Specific- "point out the offense."* Notice the verse says, "offense," singular, not plural. This is not the time to back up the dump truck and unload all of the resentment we have towards this person. It is crucial to stay on topic and stay in the present. Avoid inflammatory words that can cause the conflict to escalate. It was said of Jesus that He was full of grace and truth. When navigating through conflict, we have to practice both of these truths.

5. *Get help from one or two others.* Jesus said that if the person refuses to listen to what we have to say, that we need to take one or two people with us. These are people who love the other person and us, and want what is best for the organization.

It is important to understand that this is not talking about gossiping to another person. Joseph Stowell defines gossip as, "talking to someone about someone else who is not part of the problem or the solution."[3] If we need some help in solving the situation, then the person you talk to should be part of the healthy solution, not someone who is going to side with us.

6. *Appeal to the leadership of the church if necessary.* If the person still refuses to acknowledge and own his or her part in the conflict after taking one or two people with us, the next step is to tell it to the leaders of the church.

By doing so, we are seeking the collective wisdom of spiritual counsel as well as informing the leaders of the church of this situation. The ministry leaders are then to decide prayerfully how they will proceed. If, after seeking God about the matter, they feel led to lovingly but truthfully confront the person, the church leaders need to spend time in prayer asking God to prepare them to meet with the person.

7. *Tell it to the entire church.* If the person still refuses to listen to the leaders after three different crucial conversations, it may be necessary to inform the congregation that this person has been removed from all ministry responsibilities until he or she agrees to a restoration plan.

A restoration plan might include counseling, as well as taking steps of repentance and brokenness. It may involve family members, relatives and other people close to the person intervening on behalf of the wayward person. It may involve letting the legal system handle the matter. The leadership of the church does not have to disclose a great number of details, but rather protect the person they are attempting to correct as well as themselves.

8. *Be willing to distance yourself from the relationship.* If the person still refuses to listen, you may need to end the relationship. This means you continue to love and pray for that person, but you do so from a distance. Jesus says, *"treat that person as a pagan or a corrupt tax collector."* What does that mean? It means you treat a person as if the person was not a believer to begin with. When a person is treated like a tax collector, we still send missionaries to that person to try and win him or her back.

Sometimes we have to love someone from a distance. Just because the person has refused to repent and reconcile, we must not stop loving him or her, but we do so from a distance. We do not continue a close relationship with that person.

Several years ago a married man in our church spent an inordinate amount of time at the home of a single woman who also attended our church. His wife came to us and informed us of her concerns. We tried to gather all the facts possible from the man's wife.

After updating us that her husband continued his behavior, another pastor and I met with him and discussed the situation with him. We asked him, for the sake of his wife, his faith, and the reputation of our church, to disengage himself from this relationship. He claimed he was simply helping her out with things around the house. We cautioned him that if the behavior continued, we would have to take the next step.

A while later this man's wife called and said he was over at her house and had gone there every night that week. The other pastor and I, along with this man's wife took a drive over to this single woman's house. We knocked on the door and there was no answer. We were about to leave when the man, this single woman, and her children came walking up the street.

This husband, with a guilty look on his face, attempted to rationalize his behavior. Nothing we said broke through his denial. We informed him that the next step for us was to bring this situation to the elder board of our church.

After discussing it with our church leaders and praying about this situation, we invited this person to meet with us. He refused. We then decided our next step was to share this with the church family. We scheduled a meeting after a church service.

I remember reading a fairly lengthy description of our attempts to restore this man and his marriage. The whole time I felt sick to my stomach, not knowing how the church would respond. We shared that maybe someone in our congregation would be able to get through to this man and single parent. After we closed the meeting in prayer, I saw person after person attempt to speak truth to this man and woman about the danger of this relationship.

I wish I could write that this man and woman repented, and the man returned to his wife and worked on restoring his marriage and his family, but that's not how it turned out. A short time later, he moved out of his home and in with this woman. We continued to pray for him. The last I heard, that relationship had ended as well. As I write this, I pray for this man to experience God's healing grace in his life.

As hard as we try, our enemy will use conflict to deceive, divide, and denounce the church and her leaders. We need to be aware of his tactics and be proactive when it comes to conflict, rather than reactive.

Some Additional Things to Keep in Mind

When attempting to resolve conflict here are some additional things to keep in mind:

- *Envision what a healthy resolution looks like and pray for it.* Too often we enter conflict with no idea of what a solution looks like, other than to prove ourselves right. Warren Wiersbe once said, "Outlook often determines outcome." This can also be said of conflict. How you expect the conflict to turn out will often determine the outcome.
- *Sometimes conflict is caused by a faulty system, not a faulty person.* Often, people make the conflict personal when it is an inefficient system. Until the system gets fixed, conflicts will continue to occur. Let's assume for instance, a person signs up for something and never receives a follow up contact. The person gets really frustrated with the church and feels like he or she doesn't matter and their gifts are

not needed or welcomed. Perhaps in looking at the follow up system in place, it is discovered that the person's name was not routed to the ministry leader. Another possible cause is that no one emphasized to the leader the importance of contacting interested people promptly, and so the contact got moved to the bottom of the stack.

*   *Realize the reality of the unseen battle occurring in conflict.* Paul wrote that the other person is not our enemy. *"For we are not fighting against flesh-and-blood enemies, but against evil rulers and authorities of the unseen world...."* (Ephesians 6:12) There is a spiritual battle behind an earthly conflict. We need to be aware of it.
*   *When called upon to mediate a conflict, be careful to understand your role.* Our role is to ensure that both parties are heard, appropriate responsibility is taken, and an agreed upon course of action be taken.

Conflict can be a means to a deeper and more intimate relationship with others if we will take steps to deal with it in a proper and healthy way. I may be an optimist, but I do believe that we can learn more healthy ways to work through conflict. It is possible to grow closer and stronger in our relationships if we follow the steps Jesus laid out for us. We can still build bridges and not walls with people with whom we disagree or by whom we have been wounded.

Talk it Over:

1. Share a time when you saw conflict resolved in a healthy way. What made the difference?

2. Which principle from this chapter is the most helpful to you?

3. What can you implement starting today in your relationships to prepare you for the next time you face conflict?

Digging Deeper:

Always Resolve Everything Now: The Key to Lasting Relationships. James MacDonald. Audio series located at www.walkintheword.org

Sande, Ken. *Resolving Everyday Conflict*. Grand Rapids: Baker Books, 2011.

Chapter 16

How to Deal with Criticism

*"If you feel the need to make everyone happy you should
be a wedding planner, not a leader"*
Mark Miller

D o you remember what it was like to have pick-up games
when you were growing up? Do you recall trying to
recruit enough players to play the game? Once the teams
were formed, do you remember trying to get the team motivated and involved?

I remember one time when as kid growing up in the
Midwest, we arranged a pick-up hockey game. We rounded
up enough kids in the neighborhood to have a game and
played in my friend's driveway that had been shoveled free
of snow. The game began and we hustled and worked hard,
when all of a sudden the game stopped. What happened next
left a bunch of pre-adolescent boys standing looking at one
another. One of the players on the other team decided he
wasn't getting the puck passed to him enough. He was the
owner of the puck, so he picked it up and went home. Game
over! No more pretending to be an NHL player for me. After
being in the ministry for over three decades, I have learned
that similar things can happen to leaders if we are not cautious.

Someone can come and snatch the joy of leadership from us if we are not careful. In the last chapter we talked about how to navigate through conflict. In this chapter we want to address how you respond when the conflict is directed at you. What do you do when you become the object of others' scorn and disapproval? In this chapter, we want to prepare you for those times when they happen.

A true test of character for the leader is how he or she responds to and handles criticism. Responding to criticism can make or break the leader's effectiveness. Criticism. It's hard enough when it's justified, but when it's unfair, unkind, without warning or reason, it's worse. What can we learn from handling criticism?

Criticism is Inevitable

If there was one leader in history that was often unjustly criticized it was Jesus. Jesus gave this warning to his followers, *"Woe to you when all men speak well of you…."* (Luke 6:26) Jesus knew that if we are trying to please everyone all the time, we are probably not leading. Any time we make a decision as a leader we're opening ourselves up for disagreement. My father-in-law once said to me, "if you think you have it tough making decisions, consider a referee; every time he makes a decision, he has half the people against him."

Jesus went on to assure his future leaders, *"I have told you these things so that in me you may have peace. In this world you will have trouble. But take heart! I have overcome the world."* (John 16:33) If Jesus overcame the world, maybe we too can overcome the criticism that is intended to take us down. The potential backfiring of criticism is a risk the leader must take. When our lives are filled with ideas and dreams of what God wants, it's a risk we must be willing to take.

Dealing with Criticism

1. *Understand the importance of a gentle answer.* It's important to know the difference between responding to criticism and reacting to it. Solomon, who was considered the wisest man of his day, said, *"A gentle answer deflects anger, but harsh words make tempers flare."* (Proverbs 15:1)

   If I am to respond with a soft reply, then how do I do that? Below are some suggestions to consider.

   - Thank the person for sharing his or her criticism. This often disarms the critic when we thank him or her for sharing with us.
   - Rephrase what said back to the person. We can say something like, "What I hear you saying is..."
   - Let the person talk; don't argue with him or her.
   - Respond by saying, "This is important to you. Tell me why it means so much to you."
   - Respond by asking permission to speak about the criticism, i.e., "Can I respond to what you just said?"
   - Decide whether this criticism is really that important or not. If it's not worth dying for, you may want to think of a creative compromise.

2. *Understand the difference between constructive and destructive criticism.* Constructive criticism is intended to make us a better person. It comes from someone who believes in us and wants the best for us. Constructive criticism is best when it's specific in nature, and does not attack the whole person. The criticism that is most helpful is when a person says, "when you said or did this _____, I felt _____

_____. " This type of criticism helps us work toward improvement.

Criticism that is vague and non-specific is not helpful and often is hurtful. Destructive criticism comes in many forms. It often appears when a person attacks our character rather than our actions. Damaging criticism is often accompanied with "all or nothing thinking." This type of thinking comes to the conclusion that either a person is all right or he or she is all-wrong. Either we meet the other person's expectations all the time, or we are no good, and he or she writes us off.

Hurtful criticism can come in the form of an effort to prove oneself correct no matter the cost. The person's rationale can border on absurdity, yet they will defend their position at the expense of the relationship.

3. *Consider the character of the critic.* Ask yourself, "Is this a person whose character I respect? Does this person have my best at heart? Is he or she frequently critical? Do they have a teachable spirit, or is that person more concerned with setting others right?"

4. *Don't take yourself too seriously.* We all do and say things without thinking sometimes. We can all be accused of doing foolish things sometimes. As one pastor said, "we take God seriously, but not ourselves." Learn to laugh at yourself and keep your sense of humor.

One of the most criticized leaders in American history was Abraham Lincoln. "Lincoln carried his sense of humor straight into the White House, and it never failed him when he used it to ease the sting of political slur. Often by telling an appropriate story, he could effectively turn the tables on an antagonist." [1]

5. *Understand the power of journaling.* This can be very helpful, particularly when we are extremely frustrated. Getting our thoughts out on paper before God can provide a much needed outlet for voicing how we feel.

"One of Lincoln's most effective methods of dealing with harsh criticism was to write extended letters of refutation. Often, to vent his anger and frustration, he would sit down at his desk, compose a letter of denial and then walk away without sending it. He felt better for having stated his candor but did not want any of his angry or emotional remarks made public." [2]

6. *Pray for discernment.* Pray to the One who knows the hearts of all people. Pray for wisdom and how to respond to the criticism. We must keep our hearts teachable before God. The God who shut the mouths of lions for Daniel can also shut your critic's mouth.

A biblical example of this found in 2 Kings 19:14-19. When King Hezekiah received a critical letter from the King of Assyria named Sennacherib, he went to a quiet place and spread the letter out before the Lord. There he prayed for discernment regarding what was true and what was hype. He then prayed for protection and deliverance from his opponent.

7. *Don't allow yourself to escalate.* It is hard not to react or overreact to a critic. While there is a strong tendency to do this, it's important to practice self-control. I have to confess, when I was young in the ministry, I thought it was my responsibility to set the critic right. I quickly became defensive when criticized and convinced myself that the person was out to destroy what God was doing.

I have since realized that we can have differences of opinion with someone and not let it affect us. We can disagree about how things are done and still be friends. I think of Paul's words when he wrote, *"Never pay back evil with more evil. Do things in such a way that everyone can see you are honorable. Do all that you can to live in peace with everyone."* (Romans 12:17-18)

8. *Be confident in who you are as a person.* God has called you as a uniquely gifted leader to be used by Him to impact others. God has His thumbprint on our lives. Our identity as leaders is not in who people think we are, but in Christ.

9. *Find a godly friend with whom you can share what has happened.* Find someone who is confidential and who will pray with you, support you and will be honest with you. Find someone who has your best in mind.

10. *Concentrate on your vision and change your mistake.* If what has been said is true, then work on changing it. We must make sure, however, that we are not trying to please people in the process. We make sure we don't get sidetracked with people who are impossible to please, spending all our energy and time on trivial matters, and neglecting the work God has called us to do.

Remember that puck-snatcher? The good news is that after standing around for a few minutes in disbelief that our friend would take off with his puck, leaving us frustrated and shivering, a new kid on the block spoke up and said, I think I have a puck in my garage. After a few minutes of searching, we were back in business. The puck-snatcher was not going to hold back this group of preadolescent wannabes. We can avoid the puck-snatchers when it comes to criticism if we think proactively rather than reactively.

Criticism is inevitable, but misery is optional. I want to encourage you to learn to respond to the critics the way Jesus did. He ignored those who attempted to sidetrack Him from His mission, and focused on reaching and touching people who were lost, lonely and hurting.

Talk it Over:

1. I encourage you to look back at the list given and identify three things that you can do starting today.

2. Share a time when you were criticized. What would have been helpful to have in mind from this chapter when you experienced this criticism?

Digging Deeper:

Lotz, Ann Graham. *Wounded By God's People: Discovering How Gods' Love Heals Our Hurts*. Grand Rapids: Zondervan, 2013.

Strange, John. *Words that Sting: How to Handle Destructive Criticism Like Jesus*. Philadelphia: Ivystream Press, 2011.

Section 3

"Finding Your Unique Voice and Leading From It"

"He chose his servant David."
Psalm 78:70

Chapter 17

Discovering Your Unique S.T.O.R.Y.

"One person with passion is like forty people interested."
E.M. Forster

I grew up watching the Chicago Bulls play basketball. I recall watching Michael Jordan play in a game where he scored forty-five points, and the Bulls still lost. While it's exciting to watch a superstar perform, it's even more exciting to witness just a few years later, the Bulls winning multiple championships. What was the difference?

It wasn't until the Bulls gathered a team of players who knew exactly what their role was that the players became a high impact team. When the Bulls drafted Scottie Pippen, traded for a center named Bill Cartwright, and selected a rebounder named Horace Grant, they became a contender. It didn't stop there; they also needed a point guard who was also an excellent three-point shooter. The Bulls had John Paxson, and then Craig Hodges and Steve Kerr, who Michael Jordan could dish to if he was triple-teamed.

Each member of the Bulls' championship teams knew his role. Each of them had a part to play. You as a leader also have a unique role. No other person has your DNA, and no one has your story to discover and tell.

In this chapter, I would like to show you how to discover your unique story. Since I am a lover of acronyms, I will use S.T.O.R.Y. to help you discover how God has wired you.

S = Spiritual Gifts and Strengths

The S in STORY stands for your *spiritual gifts and strengths*. As a spiritual leader, God's Spirit has given certain abilities to you the moment you said, "yes" to Jesus. Just as you were born with certain natural abilities, you are given specific supernatural abilities when you are born again. As children of God, we are born into His family with certain abilities.

While I won't go in depth in this chapter into the spiritual gifts, each of us have been given at least one of these gifts at the moment of salvation. (1 Corinthians 12:11-14) The Apostle Peter categorized the gifts into two main categories, *speaking* gifts and *serving* gifts. (1 Peter 4:10-12) While no one has all the gifts, each believer in Jesus has at least one gift, whether it is speaking or serving.

It is important to understand what your gift is and the unique way that God has wired you, because you need to serve the majority of your time in the area(s) of your giftedness. If you lead too long outside of the area of your spiritual gifts and strengths, you will eventually experience burn out.

I encourage you to take one of the many gift inventories that are available. There are several at little or no charge. A resource I have used in training leaders is a free on-line test at www.spiritualgiftstest.com. After taking the assessment, you will be given a summary of your spiritual gifts and an explanation of each of your primary gifts.

Part of your S.T.O.R.Y also includes your *strengths*. These are the things that you naturally do, often without even thinking about them, because it's the way that your Creator has designed you. God has given you certain capabilities that you can perform confidently and with little effort. Sometimes you may even have difficulty understanding why everyone can't respond that same way you do.

"I don't have any strengths that come to mind." That was the response I received from a lady who took the leadership training class based on this material. She believed for many years that all she had to offer was a life of broken dreams, damaged relationships, and inadequacies. I encouraged her to continue with the section that was on the strengths of a leader and see what happens. She reluctantly agreed and was able to identify several hidden strengths with which God had blessed her.

When it comes to understanding your spiritual gifts and strengths, there are some things to consider when discovering and deploying these assets in your life.

• **Know your Spiritual Gifts and Strengths**

Thanks to the great work of the Gallup organization, it is now possible to discover scientifically what your top assets are as a leader. I recommend for spiritual leaders to read the book *Living Your Strengths: Discovering Your God-given Talents and Inspiring your Community* by Albert Wiseman, Donald Clifton, and Curt Liesveld. This version of the strength finder assessment is especially geared for spiritual leaders. A second version that can be used with any leadership is *Strengthsfinder 2.0* by Tom Rath.

You can access this assessment on-line or purchase the book that contains a code that will allow you to log on-line and take an assessment to determine your top five strengths. You can also upgrade the assessment to identify *all* your strengths from highest to lowest. After taking the inventory, you then can read the sections of the book that apply to your particular strengths. The authors also describe how you can use your strengths in your ministry context.

- **Serve Out of Your Strengths**

Upon identifying your gifts, it is wise to look then at your current or potential involvement in ministry. Ask yourself the questions, "Am I serving in my strength zone? Do my strengths fit with the area that I am serving?" Please keep in mind that not every job or position will allow you to serve in your strength zone one hundred percent of the time. The ratio I like to use is seventy-five, twenty-five percent of your time. There will be times when you will be asked to serve not necessarily where you are strong, but where you are needed. Let me illustrate.

If I go into the men's bathroom at our church on a given weekend and see paper towels on the floor, I can't say to myself, "Well that's not my area of strength. I really can't pick those up and throw them out." No, there is a need, and I need to respond to it as a servant leader. However, if I only serve where I am needed and not where my strengths lie, I will end up frustrated or burned out. I encourage people that if they are serving seventy-five percent of their time where they are needed and only twenty-five percent of the time where they're gifted, they need to look at changing where they serve.

Jesus told us that there are two outcomes of abiding in His leadership and staying in connection with him. First, that we will be fruitful, and second, that we would be fulfilled. (John 15: 5,11) If we are not experiencing these two dynamics, perhaps God is telling us to do something different.

A word of caution here, this does not mean that ministry won't be frustrating or unfruitful at times. Let's face it, we are in a battle for the hearts and minds of people, and at times our enemy will use whatever he can to get us discouraged and defeated. If, however, over a period of time we are becoming increasingly resentful or weary, then we need to take an inventory of our heart and ask why this is happening. I have found that when people serve in their strength zone, they are more productive and passionate. When you are doing something that deep down inside gives you fulfillment and a sense of purpose, it keeps you going when you are passing through the seasons of dryness and doubt.

- **Supercharge Your Spiritual Gifts and Strengths**

It is important to understand that our strengths become supernaturally empowered by submitting them to the strength-giver, Jesus Christ. It's possible to serve in our own strength for a while, but for anything supernatural to take place, we need to submit our strengths to God.

During my years in ministry, I have had the privilege of spending time with some very talented musicians. I have had heard some incredible stories of how God rescued them from a life of drugs and other addictions, and now they are using their strengths and talents to serve the Lord. They will tell you that playing in bars and playing in a worship service each has a completely different dynamic. It's not because the one smells like sweat, stale smoke and alcohol, but because the presence of God is felt in a profound way in a worship service. These gifted people have submitted themselves and their strengths to the Lord, and He has turbo-charged them for His glory.

One of my favorite all-time movie lines is in the film, "Chariots of Fire." Eric Lidell, who is an Olympic runner, is struggling with whether to run in the Olympics or to become a missionary. As he wrestles with this dilemma, his sister tries to persuade him to go to the mission field. Eric responds in his Scottish brogue, "When I run, I feel His pleasure." That's what it is like to serve out of a humbly submitted spirit while serving in your strengths. You sense the smile of God on your life, saying, *"Well done, my good and faithful servant."* (Matthew 25:21) This is what I created you for; it doesn't get much better than this.

When people serve in their strengths, they tend to be more productive and passionate.

- **Understand Your Greatest Strength Can Become Your Greatest Weakness**

A word of caution accompanies the use of your strengths. Understand that they can be taken to an extreme and become a liability. If your strength is more relational in orientation, you have the potential to neglect completing tasks because you are spending all your time nurturing your relationships. If you are more task-oriented in your strengths, you may lack connection with people you will need to work alongside. It is quite possible to take your strengths to an extreme and become so strength-driven you fail to be a humble leader.

The one who attempts to do ministry in his/her strengths without submitting those strengths to the Holy Spirit is like a runaway train that is heading for disaster. It is only a matter of time when that leader will either implode or explode. It is critical to remember the words of Zechariah spoken to the king of that day. *"This is what the LORD says to Zerubbabel: It is not by force, nor by strength, but by my Spirit, says the LORD of Heaven's Armies."* (Zechariah 4:6)

- **Learn to Appreciate Other's Strengths**

There have been times in my ministry that my forceful-ness as a leader has alienated some who are not in agreement with me. Over the years, God has slowly done his pruning work in my life to help me realize that others' strengths are just as important as mine.

In my current ministry setting, I work alongside some very gifted and strong leaders. They are immensely talented and motivated. One of the struggles of transitioning from a senior pastorate of a medium-sized church plant, to being on staff at a large church is realizing there are people who are more talented and gifted in certain areas than I am. Rather than resent their ideas or defend my turf, I have learned to appreciate the strengths they bring to the table. While I still find myself advocating for certain things I am passionate about, I have learned to share my thoughts and let them go. If you are to succeed as a leader, you have to separate your ideas from your ego. Too often I have gotten the two wrapped together, and when an idea was rejected, I felt rejected. I am learning that my identity is not wrapped up in my idea; it's in Jesus Christ.

- **Don't Box God In**

In all fairness, there has been some pushback about focusing only on your strengths when serving. Dr. Stephen Graves in his publication, "The Hero Leader" says, "If you do nothing but hone your strengths, at some point, you'll discover a serious lack in your ability to lead others as well." [1] He further writes, "There was a time when leaders didn't focus on what they were good at, they focused on being a complete leader." [2] There are some that believe that if we only focus and develop our strengths, we will miss out on the bigger picture of a leader; that is to adapt our style and strengths depending on the situation. Graves' point is that leaders can't afford to be a one trick pony when it comes to leadership.

It is important to understand that God is the One who gifts people with strengths.

God can do whatever He wants. He is not bound by the parameters of an assessment. While these strengths may reveal certain tendencies, keep in mind that God is the owner of all the strengths and can freely give them as He wills.

About that woman who came to me stating she didn't feel she had any strengths or much to offer. Upon taking the class and going through this section on the strengths of a leader, God did an amazing work of revealing to her that she was indeed gifted, talented and had many strengths that were beaten down by the other voices she had been hearing. The opportunity came for her to run for town councilperson in her township. She ran and was elected! If you think you don't have any strengths to offer people, your humility is one of them, but understand that God never plays enie-meanie-minie-mo with his children. He has blessed you with strengths that can become supercharged when submitted to His control. So go out and *"Be strong, in the strength of His might."* (Ephesians 6:10 N.I.V.)

Question: What are your top three spiritual gifts? What are your top three strengths?

T= Temperament

The "T" in S.T.O.R.Y represents your *temperament* or personality. Each of us has a unique personality from which we lead. While there are many resources available today to help you determine your personality type, let's look at a few of the following characteristics:

"Outgoing" or "Reserved"

This has to do with how we relate to people. Typically, outgoing people love to socialize and are energized by being around other people. They often process their thoughts verbally; they love social gatherings, and many times are the last ones to leave. They do not like being alone. They often make great salespeople and good public speakers.

Reserved people are energized by time alone. They may like people, but they love solitude. Being around others often drains them. They most likely have fewer, but deeper, relationships. These people tend to be good listeners. They process things inwardly. I have told my wife, who loves to socialize with people, "I do talk a lot, I just talk to myself." In other words, I tend to think to myself a lot and take a while to open up in a conversation. Some introverts are the best thinkers and idea people available today.

While research has been done on both personality types, I am a believer that there are degrees of both. Some are more reserved than others; some may be more outgoing than others. When it comes to leading, if you are more reserved as a leader, you may want to look for opportunities to lead that do not require you to be around a lot of unfamiliar people. We all have natural tendencies, but God can make a difference in this area. In the book of Acts, we read about the effect that the Holy Spirit had on the believers of the early church. *"And they were all filled with the Holy Spirit. Then they preached the word of God with boldness."* (Acts 4:31) Notice it doesn't say that just the extroverts were bold but rather all became bold. God can fill us with boldness regardless of our reserved tendencies.

I also think that with God's help that those who are outgoing can learn to listen and be sensitive to people's needs. When we understand our natural tendencies, we can ask God for strength to either be bold or quiet, depending on what the situation we are in requires.

Question: Are you outgoing or reserved? (Circle one)

"Planned" or "In the Moment"

This distinction has to do with how we use our time. Planned people are organized, have a to-do list, need closure on projects and work best under deadlines. It is hard for these

185

people to relax until they get their work completed. These people are more task-oriented.

The spontaneous, in the moment people are more open-ended and flexible. They can adapt as they go. It's hard for them to think a week, a month, a year in advance. They believe that relationships come first before the task. If they don't get around to doing their task, it's okay as long as the relationships in their life are healthy.

People who are in the moment probably should not be placed in charge of a project that requires multiple deadlines. However, for the relational ministries in the church, they will excel. Again, being aware of your tendencies can help you find your niche as a leader.

"Dependent on Others" or "Independent"

This difference has to do with how we get our work done. Those who are dependent upon others tend to rely on people during tough times. They need lots of guidance and supervision. These people work best in teams where they can interact and let others lead.

Question: Are you more "planned" with your time or "in the moment" (spontaneous)

Independent people don't rely on others to get the work done. They frequently plow ahead and get the job done. They tend to rely on their own resources when under pressure. Many times their thought process leads them to believe that no one can do the task quite the way they want it done, so they do it themselves. They tend to get their work done best by being alone and left to themselves. These personality types have difficulty delegating and releasing ministry to others.

Question: When you do your work are you more dependent on others or independent?

"Thinkers" or "Feelers"

This has to do with how we make decisions. People who are thinkers rely on facts and data to make wise decisions. They look at trends and patterns from the past before they move forward. They tend to be more analytical. They deal more with the real than the ideal when it comes to making decisions.

Those who are feelers tend to make decisions more intuitively than rationally. They often base their decision on how something feels to them. These people have great imaginations and want the ideal to take place. They are more futuristic in their thinking, and don't tend to look to the past to make a decision. They often act on hunches rather than facts. This does not mean that feelers don't think or thinkers never feel, but the majority of the time a leader will lean towards one of these traits or the other.

All of these personalities can appear in degrees along a continuum. It's important to understand your unique temperament so that you can find your own voice and lead from it.

It's equally important to understand that no matter what your natural personality might be, this is one area that God can give you the courage to do things differently. With Christ's help and the empowering of the Holy Spirit, you don't have to do things the way you have always done them.

On almost every personality inventory I have taken, I am considered an introvert, in large part because I am energized by times of solitude. Being around people for long amounts of time can be physically? draining. However, part of my responsibilities at the weekend services at our church is to greet people and help assist them in finding a place to connect. God has given me the courage to step outside my comfort zone and rely on His strength and not my own. I have had several people say to me, "I would never have guessed you are an introvert." The truth is that it is only because of Jesus Christ giving me the courage needed to step out of my comfort zone and reach out to others that I can connect with people.

If you are interested in looking further at your personality, I would encourage you to take both the Meyers-Briggs personality inventory as well as the DISC profile. These two personality inventories can help you realize why you often do the things you do.

Question: When you make decisions are you more of a "thinker" or a "feeler?"

O= Opportunities and Occasions

The "O" in S.T.O.R.Y. is for *opportunities and occasions.* You have been given specific experiences that have helped shape the person you are today. These include a variety of opportunities.

Some opportunities are *educational opportunities.* These include your college major, your certifications, and your favorite topics of study. God can use your educational experiences to help you determine where you lead. These add to your credibility to lead others. The Apostle Paul used his academic scholarship to lead him to places that required high credentials.

Another such category is *life occasions.* These may include marriage, raising children, spiritual experiences, lessons that you have learned from advancing in years, etc. Many of these occasions are what God uses to prepare, grow and develop your character as a leader. These life occasions are what make a great mentor, someone who has life experiences to share with those they are mentoring.

A third kind of opportunities that God gives to us are *ministry opportunities*. These are places we have served in the past, as well as those opportunities when you have been used by God to show others His love and grace in a powerful way. Sometimes by trying a ministry and discovering that it is not how you are wired, you can go on to other opportunities of service to determine where better to lead.

Finally, a kind of occasion that some of us may have had are *painful occasions*. These ordeals are those that we do not wish to go through, but looking back, we can see how God has used them to shape and prepare us for leadership. These experiences may be things we have had to overcome from our family of origin or episodes that have happened to us in adulthood. We have people in our church who are leading our grief recovery ministry; they have lost a loved one and are now helping others walk through the journey of loss. We have people leading ministries who have lost their job or a child, or a spouse. People are leading ministries who have come out of abusive and addictive relationships. God has somehow redeemed their fears, failures, and frustrations and made them caring, restorative leaders.

One of the ministries our church calls "Embrace" was born by some of my colleagues who had a heart for special needs children. They sensed that maybe there were other families who would like to attend church, but their child needed a little extra attention and grace. Thus, a ministry for special needs children was launched. Today this ministry reaches multiple families and includes an annual Christmas service called "Masterpiece" for special needs children and their families.

Another ministry that God has used in a powerful way in our church is "Celebrate Recovery." God has helped numerous people who are struggling to overcome addictions of all kinds in their life find forgiveness and strength to be released from their hurts, habits and hang-ups. Through the power of Jesus Christ and the encouragement of fellow strugglers, many are now using the pain that they have experienced to help others find freedom.

R= Resources

These are the *natural resources* with which God has blessed you. They include your skills. Just as God has given you certain spiritual gifts, He has also given you certain innate abilities that you either were born with or have developed and honed along the way. These are what we call natural talents.

Some people are talented artistically, some musically, others creatively. Certain leaders are skilled at organizing, managing finances, or using computers. Still others are good at building, repairing and painting things. Some are talented at writing, editing and producing publications. God wants to use your resources to make a difference for His kingdom.

Y= Yearnings

These have to do with the *longings of your heart*. They are areas of passion for us. We feel strongly about a certain issue, topic or area, and we feel compelled to make a contribution. An area that I am passionate about is equipping people by resourcing leaders to make new and better disciples of Jesus Christ. In my current ministry context this primarily happens with group leaders, mentors, and equipping classes that we offer.

Your yearnings can also include a certain age group you are passionate about serving. Some people are passionate about children's ministry; some are concerned about students, and still others care strongly about young marrieds. There are people who are enthusiastic about helping the poor or helping parents with teenagers. Others are passionate about men's or women's ministries.

A few years ago, I spoke with a man who offered to help serve. After the screening process, he was placed in our children's ministry, where he struggled mightily. He came to me with his struggle. Recognizing that he had gone through one of our "Discover your S.T.O.R.Y." classes, I pressed him on what was at the heart of his struggle. His spiritual gift was teaching, and he loved to teach, but his yearning was not for the first graders where he had been assigned, but rather for teaching high school boys. He related that it was during the adolescent years in his life that he came to know Jesus Christ as his leader and forgiver, and he wanted to provide the same opportunity in adolescent's lives.

When we helped him become a small group leader for our high school students, he thrived and loved it. A few years later he came to me and shared that he was thinking about going into youth ministry.

Understanding your yearnings and passion is important. It can make the difference between being energized in serving and being exhausted. When you serve in an area you are passionate about, it will sustain you through those times when life grows weary. You will understand that you can let go of a lot of things, but your area of passion is not one of them.

I love to hear people's stories. One of the areas of curiosity for me is to hear how a person's story has intersected with God's grander story of redemption. Each person you meet has a unique story to share. I want to challenge you to spend the time to discover your S.T.O.R.Y. Personally, I have committed the remainder of my life to helping people discover and develop their leadership story, and then to share it with others by developing followers of Jesus Christ.

Talk it Over:

1. What is your yearning or passion as a leader?

2. In what area of the church or community do you see the greatest need?

3. What age group or issue do you feel strongly about that gives you life and excitement?

Digging Deeper:

1. Using the acronym S.T.O.R.Y., share your personal story. Write out the word STORY vertically on a piece of paper to record your S.T.O.R.Y.

2. What area(s) of your S.T.O.R.Y. do you need to further develop?

3. What is one strength that God has given you that you can share with others?

Digging Deeper:

Rath, Tom. *Strengthfinders 2.0*. New York: Gallup Press. 2007.
Rees, Eric. *S.H.A.P.E.: Finding and Fulfilling Your Unique Purpose for Life*. Grand Rapids: Zondervan, 2004.
Winseman, Clifton and Lieveld. *Living Your Strengths: Discover Your God-Given Talents and Inspire Your Community*. New York: Gallup Press, 2004.

Helpful Websites:

www.spiritualgiftstest.com
www.uniquelyyou.com

Chapter 18

The Shadows of Leadership

"Leaders need to be students of themselves and understand the areas of their dark side."
Gary McIntosh and Samuel D. Rima Sr.

Growing up on the Southside of Chicago, I learned at an early age to fear both real and imaginary enemies. I still remember when I was around nine years old, a friend and I were walking to the store. We walked through an alley behind his house, and as we meandered through the neighborhood, my friend spotted what looked like a real handgun. He picked it up and pointed it at me. He said, "Man this looks really cool!"

After playing with it for a few minutes, we realized it probably wasn't a toy. We hid the pistol and continued on to the store. On the way home, we grabbed it and started playing with it some more. We then realized we needed tell his dad about it. Upon looking it over, his father determined it was real. He promptly called the police. We had a lot of fun riding in a police car back to where we had discovered it. On the way home the police officer put his lights and siren on for us, and he became our hero for the day.

When I was eleven we moved out of that neighborhood to a suburb. My dad's work had relocated, and he felt it was too dangerous to live where we lived. A year after we moved, a student at the elementary school I had attended was suspended. He went home found two guns in his father's gun case, went back, and shot and killed my former principal, shot and wounded the assistant principal, and finally ran out of bullets before he was abducted by teachers. This incident occurred less than a year after I had moved from that area. It was years before Columbine or any other school shootings that made the news.

I share all that to say that to say that one of the things I feared growing up were shadows. When it got dark out, my anxiety escalated. If I was walking home alone from a friend's house, I had one desire: to get home as quickly as possible. My hearing and eyesight were keenly attuned to the slightest unexpected encounter.

As leaders, we have shadows that follow us as well. We, too, need to be keenly aware that there are some predators of our souls who desire to take us out. If they can't do that, they are content with keeping us in a prison of paranoia and fear. As I have studied spiritual leaders for many years, I have found the following shadows to be struggles that may plague them.

Driven Leaders

These leaders are driven to succeed in their ministry. They have a hard time saying no to people. Underneath their busy schedules is a need to please others caused by a fear of failure and rejection. In his book, *"Ordering your Private World,"* Gordon MacDonald makes the distinction between leaders who are *driven* and those who are *called*. He gives these descriptions of the persons who are driven.

- They are abnormally busy.
- They are most often only gratified by accomplishment.
- They are usually highly competitive.
- They are often characterized by limited or undeveloped people skills.
- They are often irritable, and can possess "a volcanic force of anger."[1]

Discouraged Leaders

The hurts and disappointments of ministry, the sleepless nights thinking about situations in the church, unresolved conflict, unmet budgets, and the busyness of people's demands on our time can all take their toll. The result is that discouragement can take up residence in the leader's heart. If it is not addressed and counteracted, it can lead to depression. The most joyful job in the world can soon be blanketed by a hopeless funk that comes over us like a fog bank that rolls in unannounced. We become resentful of people and their problems. Discouragement left unchecked can often lead to the next shadow of leadership.

Distant Leaders

Distant leaders are those who, because of the hurts and wounds of ministry, have closed their heart to people. Some people who are like this isolate themselves from other people, even those closest to them. They emotionally stiff-arm anyone who gets close, and they keep everyone at a distance. The challenge for these leaders is that to authentically shepherd people, we have to get close to them. To speak into their lives, we have to know what they are facing and feeling. Distant leaders have a difficult time maintaining close relationships. They have come to the conclusion that they must lead people from a distance. The problem with that approach is we will never discover what people are struggling with if we don't spend time with them. We may hold a type of positional leadership over them, but there will be no personal leadership if we close off our heart to people.

Distracted Leaders

These leaders have too many commitments vying for their attention. These distractions may be good, bad or neutral in nature. It is problematic for them to devote themselves fully to their leadership responsibilities due to the multiple distractions pulling them away from attending to their important leadership tasks. They often start things and don't complete them. They may procrastinate on developing and communicating the vision and values of the organization. Distracted leaders often have difficulty staying focused during their quiet time if they even have one. They may go through the routine of devotions, but the relationship with Christ suffers due to a crowded heart.

Jesus put it this way in the parable He told about the four types of soil;

He mentioned the seed that fell on the thorny ground. He explained, *"But all too quickly the message is crowded out by the worries of this life, the lure of wealth, and the desire for others things, so no fruit is produced."* (Mark 4:19)

Deceived Leaders

These leaders have somehow been led to believe that they can compartmentalize their leadership. They are sure that they can live one way in public and another privately.

We have all heard about leaders who were forced to resign because their private and public lives were so incongruent it eventually became public knowledge. I have met with several leaders over the years who were somehow convinced that they would not get caught. They appeared outwardly to be successful, but inwardly and privately they made multiple compromises. They thought it would not damage their ministry, and in some distorted way, they believed they deserved to act out.

James, the brother of Jesus, wrote about the progression of deception. *"Temptation comes from our own desires, which entice us and drag us away. These desires give birth to sinful actions. And when sin is allowed to grow, it gives birth to death." (James 1:14-15)* Notice the development of deception written here.

First, is the *curiosity* stage. All sin begins in the mind as Satan makes us curious for the things that are harmful to us. Second comes the *enticement* stage. This is the stage when the pleasure of sin is offered as something so attractive and satisfying that we want to pursue it with our mind and emotions. Warren Wiersbe says, "Temptation always carries with it some bait that appeals to our natural desires. There is an outward lure and an inward lust"[1]

The next stage is the *conception* stage. When our weak will yields to lust, and we give in to it, sin is conceived. Lust is allowed to take over our will. Our thinking has become clouded, and we become obsessed with fulfilling our desires.

The fourth stage is the *birth of sin* stage. This stage is when the act of sin is carried out. Both Satan and our sin nature entice us, but it is still our choice that makes sin become a reality in our life.

The fifth stage is the *sin maturing* stage. In this stage, sin is allowed to reside in our lives. Instead of confessing our sin and forsaking it, we let it remain. Someone has put it this way: "Thoughts lead to actions, actions lead to habits, habits lead to more action, more action leads to disaster."

The final stage is the *disaster* stage. Once sin forms into a habit, it will eventually lead to disaster. The word death in this means separation. Sin separates us from fellowship with

God, and with other people in our lives. Here are some examples of separation from God:

- Guilt
- Slavery
- Low self-worth
- Constant worry and fear of being found out
- Broken relationships
- Wasted time
- Continual anger, frustration and resentment

Defensive Leaders

These leaders feel the need to be right all of the time. When confronted with a problem, they immediately feel the need to defend what they did or said. Rather than listening and clearing up any misunderstanding, they further compound the problem by proving themselves right. Their self-justification makes it difficult for people to come to them for clarification and confrontation.

I understand this kind of leader because for years, I took this approach. I thought it was my job as a pastor to convince the dissenters they were wrong. My dark side of leadership is what Gary McIntosh and Samuel D. Rima Sr., in their book, *"The Dark Side of Leadership,"* call, "the paranoid leader."[2] My own insecurities and lack of self-esteem, resulted in many times winning the debate but losing the relationship. I had to learn that not everyone who confronts us is out to destroy us.

In recent years, I have learned that I need to listen and respond graciously to criticism rather than follow my flesh and react defensively. I can thank the person for sharing things with me. I can commend them for coming to me with it. We can work on what Covey calls a "third alternative."

Demanding Leaders

These leaders are what are known as "control freaks" or "micro-managers." These people use their positional authority to demand that people follow them. They will use the organizational chart in such a way as to demand certain things from their followers. I have seen pastors use the Bible in such a way as to demand certain things from people. Demanding leaders believe they are the leader, and their followers are servants. Those under them are not just to serve God, but they are to serve them as well. When someone questions a decision, demanding leaders will often pull the "I'm the leader" card.

This can be difficult at times for leaders because by definition, leaders are the ones who take charge. They are the ones who make things happen. They are the ones who are a catalyst for change. Leaders have the responsibility to see that results happen in a productive way. Leaders have the responsibility for making sure the vision of the organization stays on track.

It is important, however, for leaders to guard against a demanding demeanor. The Apostle Paul wrote, *"Love does not demand its own way."* (1 Corinthians 13:5) One way to do this is to learn to serve alongside those who follow us.

It is also important to realize that when we release ministry to others, we have to allow a margin for them to use their own creativity, gifting, and personality to accomplish the task.

Depleted Leaders

These leaders are simply going through the motions. The passion and enthusiasm for what they do are no longer present. In many cases, this happens after a season of busyness and high demands or a major event. The result is they are depleted physically, emotionally and spiritually.

It is important to realize that all leaders go through times of depletion, exhaustion, and loneliness. It is during these times that self-care is critical. It is important to look ahead at our schedule for those seasons when we are crazy busy, and be sure to schedule renewal time following them.

Recently, I shared with our men about recognizing weariness. I said, "The quality of our life is determined by how we manage and respond to weariness." I then gave them following weariness test, which may also be helpful to you:

1. How are your joy and gratitude?
2. How is your frustration level lately?
3. Are you enjoying or enduring life these days?
4. Do you have genuine compassion for broken people?
5. Do you hear the still small voice of God regularly?
6. Is God real in your life, or are you just going through the motions?
7. Are you sleeping well and getting exercise?

How to Overcome Your Leadership Shadows

Now that we have taken a look at some of the shadows of leadership, how do we rise above them? What can we do to guard ourselves against allowing the shadows to overtake us and keep us living in fear?

- Turn towards the light. The way we lose our fear of the shadows is by turning towards the light. The Apostle John wrote, *"But if we are living in the light, as God is in the light, then we have fellowship with each other, and the blood of Jesus, his Son, cleanses us from all sin."* (1 John 1:7) Thank God that through His Spirit, He has revealed the shadow in your life.
- Return to your first love. If we want what we once had, we have to do what we once did. That is true in both our earthly relationships as well as our relationship with Christ. The church at Ephesus was known

for hard work and their patient endurance. They were not tolerant of false teachers and immoral people. But John writes that Jesus had one criticism of them. *"You don't love me or each other as you did at first!"* (Revelation 2:4) They had neglected the things that caused them to fall in love with Jesus in the first place. In the next section, we are going to look at some of the things we can do to keep our hearts from growing cold.

- Learn to S.T.A.N.D. F.I.R.M. Several years ago I taught that a way to overcome temptation and the shadows in our life is to learn to S.T.A.N.D F.I.R.M. This acronym stands for:

S- *State Scripture out loud.* There is something powerful in quoting Scripture either by reading it or from memory.

T- *Turn to God in prayer.* Prayer is the means by which we touch the heart of God and find the strength to overcome the darkness in our lives. Sometimes the only way out of a situation is to cry out to God in prayer and ask Him for the strength to say no.

A- *Avoid tempting situations.* Years ago there was a song I used to love written by a man named Rich Mullins. The title of the song was, "We're Not as Strong as We Think We Are." We need to avoid those situations where we are vulnerable to giving in to our shadows.

N- *Nourish your relationships.* The enemy of your soul wants to isolate you and have you believe that no one understands and no one cares. If he can convince you that you are all alone, he has half the battle won. The Apostle Paul wrote, *"The temptations in your life are no different from what others experience. And God is faithful. He will not allow the temptation to be more than you can stand. When you are tempted, he will show you a way out so that you can endure."* (1 Corinthians 10:13)

Having the support of a godly friend who you can turn to during times of celebration as well as challenge can help you overcome your shadows. Knowing there is someone you can call, text or pray with can provide strength that is beyond you.

D- *Declare your victory through Christ.* Christ gave His life to free us, not from the presence of sin, but from the penalty and power of it. We will never be completely free from the presence of sin on this side of heaven. But we are freed from the penalty and power of sin in our lives. We no longer have to sin. We now, through Christ, have the power to say no to the shadows that lurk in our path.

F-*Flee.* Remove yourself from tempting situations. Not allowing yourself to associate with compromising places and people can help you overcome the dangers of your dark side. Paul wrote to Timothy, a young leader in the church at Ephesus, *"Flee the evil desires of youth and pursue righteousness, faith, love and peace, along with those who call on the Lord out of a pure heart."* (2 Timothy 2:22 N.I.V.)

I- *Interrupt your thinking with the truth.* Satan loves to hide the consequences from us. If he can convince us that we owe it to ourselves to indulge, the birth of sin has begun. Once we start listening to the shadows, we begin following them. If we don't do something to change our thinking, we can easily find ourselves saying and doing things that are damaging to others and us.

One way to do this is to write out truths cards and carry them with you. These cards can easily be made with a three by five inch index card. When you discover a truth about who you are in Christ or what He says about your shadow, write it out and carry it with you. Reminding yourself regularly of God's truth can help both renew your mind as well as resist the Devil in your life.

R- *Rely on God's Strength, not your own.* I have shared with people that we don't need willpower in our lives; we need "won't power." If you rely on your own strength to fight the battle, you will end up defeated and frustrated. King Jehoshaphat faced an invasion by three different nations that were coming against him. The fear of defeat was overwhelming. But God came to the King and said these words that he relayed to the people of God. *"Listen, all you people of Judah and Jerusalem! Listen, King Jehoshaphat! This is what the LORD says: Do not be afraid! Don't be discouraged by this mighty army, for the battle is not yours, but God's."* (2 Chronicles 20:15) May God grant us the same insight when we are staring down our shadows.

M-*Meditate on the truth.* We must change our "stinkin thinkin", and replace it with the truth of who we are in Christ and what He says about us. It is always helpful to memorize God's Word and meditate on it during our day-to-day activity.

We all have shadows. If you don't think you have a dark side, re-read the section of this chapter on the deceived leader. Effective leaders are those who can recognize their shadow and take steps to expose it to the light, where it loses its power. As important as it is to lead others, we must first lead ourselves as well. Being aware of our tendencies may not eliminate mistakes, but they can help us as leaders stop them before they become dominant in our lives.

Talk it Over:

1. Which of the above leadership shadows do you struggle with the most?

2. What can you do to guard against these shadows?

3. What is one thing you can take away that will help you slay your shadows?

Digging Deeper:

McIntosh, Gary and Samuel D. Rima Sr. *The Dark Side of Leadership*. Grand Rapids: Baker Books, 2007.
Scazzero, Peter. *The Emotionally Healthy Leader: How Transforming Your Inner Life Will Deeply Transform Your Church, Team and the World*. Grand Rapids: Zondervan, 2015.

Section 4

"Exercising Heart Healthy Habits"

"He cared for them with a true heart."
Psalm 78:72

Chapter 19

The Heart of a Leader

*"It's not just our physical heart that is important; espe-
cially as leaders, our spiritual heart is equally important."*
Michael Hyatt

A few years ago both my parents had open-heart surgery
within three months of each other. While visiting with
doctors and surgeons, I learned a lot about the human heart,
more than I wanted to know. Following my dad's surgery,
multiple complications occurred which almost led to his
death several times. What was supposed to be a four-hour
surgery turned into a sixteen-hour touch-and-go situation
where they reopened his heart three times to stop the bleeding.

Being a first-hand witness to this drama in real life set me
on a path to discovering the health of my own heart. I learned
that I need to have regular blood panels to make sure my indicators are in the healthy range. I also learned the importance
of eating healthy food as well as de-stressing through exercise and prayer on a regular basis.

When it comes to the Christian life, having a healthy
heart is important as well. It is important to monitor our spiritual heart and watch the indicators that are warnings we are
heading into dangerous territory.

What Do We Mean by the "Heart."

The word "heart" is used in the Bible 765 times. It was used most frequently to describe the center of one's being. The word "heart" in the Bible is the place where we desire, deliberate and decide. It is the place where our *desires* dwell. We talk about loving God with all our heart. That means we desire God more than anything else in life.

The word also describes the place where we *deliberate*. It involves our thoughts and reasoning. *"Trust in the LORD with all your heart and lean not on your own understanding; in all your ways submit to him, and he will make your paths straight."* (Proverbs 3:5-6 N.I.V.) Solomon is stating that we are not to rely on our own intuition or ingenuity but to seek the "mind of Christ." This part of our heart has been called the "thought life." It is the place where our self-talk resides.

Finally, the word "heart" is also that place where we *decide,* where we choose. It was said of Pharaoh that he *"But when Pharaoh saw that there was relief, he hardened his heart and would not listen to Moses and Aaron, just as the Lord had said."* (Exodus 8:15 N.I.V.) In other words, he decided not to let the Israelites leave. Eventually, we know that his decisions led to a hardness of heart that was beyond repair.

The "heart" in the Bible includes the mind, the emotions, and the will. That's why it is so important to keep our hearts healthy and strong. As spiritual leaders, particular things will cause our hearts to grow cold if we allow them.

To have a healthy heart, we need to *review* and *renew* what's in our heart on a frequent basis. When we discover those things that restrict the blood flow from God's heart to ours, we need to reject and replace them with God's truth.

"Guard your heart for it affects everything you do." Proverbs 4:23

The word "guard" means to pay close attention to what is in our heart. We must review and renew our heart on a regular basis. Jesus put it this way, *"For out of the abundance of the heart the mouth speaks."* (Matthew 12:34 E.S.V.) Have you ever found yourself saying, "I can't believe I said that! Where did that come from?" It came from what's in your heart. Whatever is allowed to live and linger in our hearts will eventually emerge.

"Our Lifestyle is a Result of our Heart-Style."

I want to spend the remainder of this chapter focusing on some heart issues that are particularly dangerous for spiritual leaders. If these practices are allowed to take up residence, we can easily move into the danger zone in our health as leaders.

With each risk area, I will propose a heart healthy practice that will counteract the hazard. I want to encourage you to use this chapter as a guide to review and renew your heart as a leader on a regular basis.

1. *Fear*

As spiritual leaders, many fears can enter our heart. We must recognize them, reject them and replace them with healthy habits.

> *"So we say with confidence, 'The Lord is my helper; I will not be afraid. What can mere mortals do to me?'"* (Hebrews 13: 6)

Fear believes that the worst is going to happen. Fear comes down to what we are telling ourselves about God and the situation we are thinking about. There are all kinds of concerns that leaders have. Here are some of them:

- Fear of rejection
- Fear of failure

- Fear of intimacy- because we have been hurt by people we have trouble opening our heart to others.
- Fear of not having enough
- Fear of losing the favor of people
- Fear that staff are undermining our authority
- Fear of the future
- Fear of doing the right thing

"Fear of man will prove to be a snare, but whoever trusts in the LORD is kept safe." (Proverbs 29:25)

Heart Healthy Practice: Confidence

We need to remind ourselves that God is the One who calls us to this task, and He is with us. The writer of Hebrews tells us the Lord is our helper, and we don't have to be afraid. People can wound us, and Satan can accuse us, but God is with us and will see us through. (Hebrews 13:5-6)

It's important to know that if God has called us to a leadership task, He will supply the grace to help us accomplish the task. We can lead knowing that Jesus, who gave His leaders the commission to *"make disciples,"* also said He would be with us *"until the end of the age."* (Matthew 28:19-20)

God's instructions to Joshua were to be confident in the presence and promise of God. *"This is my command—be strong and courageous! Do not be afraid or discouraged. For the LORD your God is with you wherever you go."* (Joshua 1:9)

We need to lead with God-confidence, realizing that God has promised to be with us, working through our weaknesses to demonstrate His power. He knows our fears, frustrations, and failures, yet still loves and chooses to use us.

I want to encourage you to memorize Hebrews 13:6 and Joshua 1:9. When you become afraid, I want to challenge you to claim these verses as a leader. As we fill our minds with

God's truth and choose to live by faith and not fear, we begin to see fear diminish in our hearts.

2. *Greed*

> *"Keep your lives free from the love of money and be content with what you have, because God has said, 'Never will I leave you; never will I forsake you.'"* Hebrews 13:5

Greed is an excessive desire, especially for wealth or possessions. Greed is our ambitions on steroids. It is the unhealthy obsession with longing for what we don't have. It is not wrong to wish or have goals and aspirations as a leader, but we can cross a line into an unhealthy zone of lusting for more. Unfortunately, greed is one of those things that can enter the heart of a leader without making a lot of noise until it's too late.

Greed usually begins with our attitude. We tell ourselves, "we deserve better than this!" which often leads to us pursuing things that we can't afford or are harmful to us. It is an elusive search for meaning and fulfillment apart from what we have and our relationship to God.

It's possible, as leaders, to let money become the focal point of our life and ministry. The Bible does not say money is the root of all evil, it says, *"the love of money is the root of all evil."* (1 Timothy 6:10)

I can tell you from experience that the times I struggled most with the love of money is when I had very little of it. It was during those times I would obsess and worry endlessly about what I didn't have and what others had. You don't have to have a lot to "love money."

Jesus put it this way, *"Be on your guard against all kinds of greed; life does not consist in an abundance of possessions."*

(Luke 12:15 N.I.V.) Greed can take many forms. Consider the following:

- Constantly dealing with "when and then" thinking. When I get this, then I will be happy.
- Going deeper and deeper into debt.
- Having to have the latest and best, not because of its usability, but because of its status.
- Going to places on the internet that are damaging to yourself and others.
- Living for more-more possessions, more power, more pleasure.
- Eating unhealthy foods and becoming obese.
- Not being honest on an expense report or with our taxes.

Have I said enough? Greed is damaging to our heart. I believe that it is going to become increasingly harder to combat against greed in the years ahead. With all of the persuasive messages we are faced with daily, it is critical that we combat against greed in our lives with the provision that God gives us.

Heart Healthy Practice: Contentment

We need to learn to be satisfied, thankful and grateful for what we have. We need to comprehend how fortunate we are to be in Christ.

Andy Stanley says, "If you make $37,000.00 a year or more you are in the top four percent of wage earners in the world."[1] If you make this amount or more, congratulations! You are one of the richest people on the planet.

Contentment is learning that the best stuff in life is not stuff. Contentment loosens the grip of greed on our heart. Someone recently challenged me to start my day listing twenty things I am thankful for each day. He said this practice changed his perspective on life. Contentment in Christ keeps us from comparing ourselves with others.

Isn't it interesting that we typically compare ourselves to those who have more than us, not less? We tend to measure our success by those who appear to have more of what is important to us than those who have less. One way we can battle greed is to volunteer to serve in a soup kitchen for the poor, disadvantaged, and homeless, and spend time talking to those we are serving. We will come to appreciate the things we have in a new way.

A final way to practice contentment and break the grip of greed is through *generosity*, learning to give and bless others. By giving to God and His mission, and helping those in need, we free our hearts from the hold that greed has on us.

I have had pastors tell me that they don't have to give in the offering because it's recycled money, meaning it's just going to come back. Others have said since they volunteer their time, they don't need to tithe or give.

By taking this approach, not only do we rob God of what rightfully belongs to Him, but we also set ourselves up for greed to become a god in our life. God has designed for contentment to control our hearts and greed to be broken when we practice generosity in His name.

3. Anger

"My dear brothers and sisters, take note of this:
Everyone should be quick to listen, slow
to speak and slow to become angry,
because human anger does not produce the
righteousness that God desires." (James 1:19-20 N.I.V.)

We all deal with anger in different ways. Some of us are aggressive in our expression of anger; some are passive-aggressive. Unrestrained anger has caused a lot of problems for leaders. Moses lost his integrity because of his anger. God told Moses to speak to the rock and it would produce water for God's people. Moses was so frustrated with the complaining that was going on, that in his anger he struck the rock, twice, and it produced water. (Numbers 20:1-11) *"But the LORD said to Moses and Aaron, 'Because you did not trust me enough to demonstrate my holiness to the people of Israel, you will not lead them into the land I am giving them!'"* (Numbers 20:12)

Anger can manifest itself in a lot of ways. Consider some of these subtle and not-so-subtle expressions:

- Frustration with the people we lead
- Irritation by irresponsibility or lack of commitment
- Gossip
- Outburst of anger
- Sabotaging someone's effort
- Procrastination
- Bitterness
- Sarcasm
- Harsh words
- Slander
- Envy
- Being taken for granted
- Fear

On a personal level, for years as a leader this area has been one of both testing and weakness. I have on more than one occasion expressed my frustration and irritation with people in a way that has damaged my credibility. When I was younger, I thought the way to convince someone who disagreed with my leadership was to set them straight. While most of my confrontations were in private, and not violent, nevertheless they were not honoring to God at best.

I justified my anger by telling myself that Jesus got angry. He went into the temple and turned over tables and drove out the moneychangers. I certainly have not gone to that extreme.

One day I re-read the account of Jesus driving out the vendors and something jumped off the page at me. I read, *"In the Temple area he saw merchants selling cattle, sheep and doves for sacrifices; he also saw dealers at tables exchanging foreign money. Jesus made a whip from some ropes and chased them all out of the Temple. He drove out the sheep and cattle, scattered the moneychangers' coins over the floor, and turned over their tables."* (John 2:14-15)

Did you see it? It says, "Jesus made a whip." This act wasn't some impulsive explosion of anger, it wasn't a spontaneous knee-jerk reaction to what He saw going on around Him, He made a whip!

Heart Healthy Habit: Christ-control

How do we learn to whip our anger? How do we learn through Christ's help to make a whip when we get angry? Let me use the acronym W.H.I.P to give you four points.

W- *Wait before responding*

> *"A fool gives full vent to his anger.*
> *But a wise person holds it back." (Proverbs 29:11)*

Would you agree with me that our first response is usually not the best one? Our initial response is usually the one that gets us into trouble. Thomas Jefferson said, "When angry count to ten; if still angry, count to one hundred."

As we take the time to cool down and wait before responding, we can ask ourselves, "Why am I angry?" "What is causing my anger?" Usually, anger can be traced back to triggers that are centered in frustration, hurt or fear.

Identifying the cause of the anger can help us counteract it. The only way we can do this is to take a time out, step back and cool down.

H- *Have a good reason to be angry*

Not all anger is wrong, it's the expression of that anger that may or may not be wrong. Here is my definition of anger. "Anger is a God-given emotion of strong displeasure triggered by a sense of injustice which can be expressed in a constructive or destructive manner."

Anger is God-given. One of the ways we are made in the image of God is that we get angry. God Himself gets angry and He created us with the ability to feel anger the way He does.

A sense of injustice can trigger it. That's why we get angry. We feel that an injustice has been done. We get angry because we want to right a wrong that has been committed from our perspective. The problem is that our perspective may not always be accurate.

Finally, anger can be expressed in a constructive or destructive manner. Often it's not the emotion of anger that is wrong; it's the expression. Our anger becomes wrong when it turns to retaliation or defensiveness. When we seek revenge, anger becomes adversarial.

Jesus had a good reason to be angry. The place where people were to connect with God had become a place of distraction and greed. The place where people came to worship God had become a tourist trap where visitors were being ripped off.

I- *Interrupt the anger by forgiving*

It is important to learn to forgive the person who offends us. Forgiveness is not the same as trusting someone again.

Trust takes time to build and rebuild. It begins with forgiveness and grows with consistent behavior, not perfection.

Forgiveness is not the same as saying nothing happened or minimizing the offense. Forgiveness first and foremost is a decision of the will. The emotion of forgiveness may not be present at the moment we decide to forgive.

We may say, "They don't deserve to be forgiven." They may not have even acknowledged any wrongdoing. That might be entirely correct. At the core of forgiveness is giving someone what he or she doesn't deserve.

The word "forgiveness" in the Bible comes from the same root as the word "grace." Grace is defined as "undeserved kindness" or "unmerited favor." By forgiving someone, we are giving them what they need, not what they deserve.

In forgiving, we are letting go of the hurt and not expecting anything in return. We are releasing our right to get even or to expect that person to suffer for what they did. Most importantly, forgiving another is really freeing ourselves more than anyone else.

Release the Prisoner

Release the Prisoner!
Release or he will die.
Release the prisoner?
Where's justice, my reply
Release the prisoner!
I heard again the cry.
Release the prisoner!
With grace my sole supply,
I released the prisoner
And saw that it was "I."[2]

If anyone had the right be angry for the injustice done to Him, it was Jesus. Beaten, spit upon, mocked, whipped, He had every reason to hold onto His right to be angry and hurt. But on the cross, He cried, *"Father, forgive them, for they don't know what they are doing."* (Luke 23:34)

P -*Pray for Strength, and Surrender Your Anger to God*

Often the cause of our anger is that we want to control someone or something. We want to control their response. We want them to come crawling on their knees begging for our forgiveness. Unfortunately, it is unrealistic to expect another person to humble himself or herself enough for us to forgive him/her.

God wants us to surrender to His control, to let go of the hurt and surrender the control of our life to Him.

4. *Envy*

Envy can appear in a variety of ways. It most frequently happens by comparing and complaining. When we compare ourselves to others, we seldom win. It is our natural tendency to compare our wealth, our position, our people, and our ministry to those who have more than less.

Envy also happens when we begin to complain about what we don't have, about how easy others have it, and how we are struggling with life. We can go on social media and see what others are getting to do and easily feel like we are missing out.

We become like the people of God who had come out of four hundred years of slavery being forced to hard labor with very few resources. When times got rough in the wilderness, instead of trusting God they wanted to return to their slavish conditions. It all started with their complaining heart attitude.

James tells us what the source of many conflicts come from; *"You are jealous of what others have, but you can't get it, so you fight and wage war to take it away from them.*

Yet you don't have what you want because you don't ask God for it. And even when you ask, you don't get it because your motives are all wrong- you want only what will give you pleasure." (James 4:2-3) All those reading these words said- OUCH!

The danger of envy is that it robs us of the new work that Christ wants to do in us today. He has new lessons, provisions and grace He wants to give to us each day, but if we continue comparing and complaining, we will not experience the goodness of God in our life.

Heart Healthy Habit- Celebrating

We need to learn to celebrate. This habit of celebrating is two-dimensional. First, we need to learn to celebrate what God is doing in others, such as when God answers prayer and when God blesses someone else more than us.

I have a confession to make. I have a hard time celebrating when someone does the same thing as I do, but better. Whether it's speaking, leading, or serving, it takes a lot of grace for me to be happy for them. But I am learning that if my heart is to be free, I have to celebrate what God is doing in and through that person.

A second way that we need to learn to celebrate is by reveling in what God has done in our life. We give thanks for the many ways that God has chosen to enrich our lives- spiritually, relationally, materially, physically, and vocationally.

5. *Guilt*

Someone has said that when we attempt to cover up our guilt that it is like trying to keep a bunch of beach balls submerged under water. Eventually, they come up to the surface and become public. Our tendency is to grab it and push it back down under the water.

Guilt is caused by wrongdoing. Sin occurs in two ways. There are sins of commission which are those sins we willfully and knowingly commit against God and others. We sin when we know better but choose to do it regardless; we are saying to God, "I don't really believe that You know what's best for me; let me help You out."

Sin can also occur by omission. *"Remember, it is sin to know what you ought to do and then not do it."* (James 4:17) When we know what the loving thing to say or do is but we refuse to do it, the result is sin.

<u>Heart Healthy Habit</u>- Confession

God has said that the habit we need to develop to attack guilt is confession. *"If we claim we have no sin, we are only fooling ourselves and not living in the truth. But if we confess our sins to him, he is faithful and just to forgive our sins and cleanse us from all wickedness."* (*1* John 1: 8-9)

I don't believe that God designed us to walk around feeling guilty all the time. To me, guilt is like that check engine light. It informs us that something is not right, that we are not getting the power we need to function properly. But just as that trouble light doesn't permanently stay on, I don't think God desires for us to live life feeling guilty all of the time. Guilt is the indicator light that something is not right. Confession is the bottle of fuel injector cleaner. Agreeing with God that we have committed or omitted something that grieves His heart restores the power to our life.

6. *Pride*

As spiritual leaders, one of the constant heart issues that must be countered is pride. When we are given the position or title as leader, it is possible to think that we can lead in our strength and know-how. When we open the door to pride, we say hello to many of the heart-damaging issues that we have already examined.

We can easily downshift from God's power to our own, and wonder why things are not as they should or could be.

Pride wears many different outfits. It can come from insecurity, not knowing who we are or our ultimate role. We can begin to crave attention, affirmation and the applause of people. I once had a professor state this about pride, "empty dump trucks make the loudest noise." In other words, when we are empty on the inside, we will crave things that will prop us up the outside.

One of my favorite verses is found in Proverbs 27:2, *"Let someone else praise you, not your own mouth- a stranger, not your own lips."* This verse tells us that we should let someone else do the boasting about our leadership, not ourselves.

Pride can also attempt to control. The more out of control life becomes, the more we grasp for control. Pride causes us to think that we can control people, circumstances and outcomes. Pride causes us to assume the role of God in life when we attempt to control the outcomes that ultimately He alone can control.

King Saul began as a strong leader. But because of his pride, insecurity and desire to control David, he ended in ruins. His pride caused him to "help" out the prophet Samuel and God. The consequence was that he surrendered his leadership and become a one-generation leader.

Pride can manifest itself through overconfidence when we assume that we can handle a situation. There is a difference between cockiness and confidence. Cockiness is an arrogance that is based on self; confidence is an assurance that God is with us and for us. They are polar opposites.

Pride can come through when we refuse to admit failure. We become defensive and distant rather than humble and teachable. When Adam and Eve displayed the first act of pride, the result was they became defensive and distant from

God. When God confronted them with their actions, rather than admit their wrongdoing, they blamed and shamed. They made excuses and minimized their wrong choice. The result is their pride problem was passed down to all of us today.

No wonder the Apostle Paul instructed the believers at Colossae with these words; *"Since God chose you to be the holy people he loves, you must clothe yourselves with tender-hearted mercy, kindness, humility, gentleness, and patience. Make allowance for each other's faults, and forgive anyone who offends you. Remember, the Lord forgave you, so you must forgive others. Above all, clothe yourselves with love, which binds us all together in perfect harmony."* (Colossians 3:12-14)

Heart Healthy Habit- Humility

Humility is not thinking less of ourselves; it's thinking of ourselves less. Peter made it clear in his instructions to spiritual leaders, *"And all of you, dress yourselves in humility as you relate to one another, for 'God opposes the proud but gives grace to the humble.' So humble yourselves under the mighty power of God, and at the right time he will lift you up in honor."* (1 Peter 5:5-6)

Humility does not believe that we are nobody and a nothing. Jesus did not die for nobodies and nothings. Humility is seeing ourselves as God sees us, nothing more and nothing less.

God is present in a powerful way when we practice humility. He says, *"The high and lofty one who lives in eternity, the Holy One, says this: 'I live in the high and holy place and with those whose spirits are contrite and humble. I restore the crushed spirit of the humble and revive the courage of those with repentant hearts.'"* (Isaiah 57:15)

I am one of those weird persons who love to power-wash things. When I fire up my power washer, I've been known to pressure wash concrete, windows, and even my dog. There is nothing quite like the look and smell of something that has been power scrubbed.

Recently, I took with me on stage a power washer to demonstrate what God wants to do in our hearts (no, I didn't hook up the water). I shared that God cleanses us the moment we acknowledge our need for Him and place our trust in the finished work of Christ, but He continues to do it each time we practice these heart healthy habits. He pressure washes our souls with His grace and mercy.

Will you allow God to turn on His power washer in your heart today and let Him get rid of the debris that has attached to your soul? As God promises and provides cleansing there will be people around you who say, "There is nothing quite like the look and smell of a divinely cleansed person."

I challenge you to read the following verse slowly and thoughtfully. Now that we have read this chapter, let's make these words of David our own prayer:

"Search me, O God and know __my heart__; test me and know my anxious thoughts. Point out anything in me that offends you, and lead me along the path of everlasting life."
(Psalm 139:24)

Challenges to consider:

- Pray Psalm 139:24 every day for a week, asking God to reveal any of the six heart damaging practices, and asking Him to power wash them from your heart.
- Take one of these areas each day for the next week and ask God to show you any ways that your heart is growing cold toward Him and others. When He reveals them to you, take time to release them to God.
- Look back on the verses used in this chapter, put them on index cards and begin reviewing and using them

to remind you of what God desires for us as spiritual leaders.

Talk it Over:

1. Which of the above heart stoppers do you struggle with the most?

2. What have you done recently to encourage a healthy heart?

3. Were you able to take the above challenges? Why? Why not?

Digging Deeper:

McNeal, Reggie. *A Work of Heart: Understanding How God Shapes Spiritual Leaders:* San Francisco: Jossey-Bass, 2011.

Stanley, Andy. *Enemies of the Heart: Breaking Free from the Four Emotions that Control You.* Colorado Springs: Multnomah Books, 2011.

Chapter 20

Heart Healthy Habits Part 1

Exercises of Engagement
"Sow a thought, reap an action,
Sow an action, reap a habit,
Sow a habit, reap a lifestyle,
Sow a lifestyle reap a destiny."
Ralph Waldo Emerson

I have been a member at a local gym for several years. While I have not always been as consistent as I would like, I do hit the gym between three and four times a week. For years, I worked out on the same machine every time I went. While I'm sure the elliptical machine was good for my heart, it was not giving me the results I desired. I found that it began to take longer and longer to see any reduction in weight.

Recently, I decided to mix up my work out. Having the same amount of time to exercise, I try to do a different routine each week. I do some strength training, stretching, and cardio on different days. I am slowly beginning to see my spare tire deflate and my triple chin move toward a twin chin.

In this chapter, and the next, I want to share with you some spiritual workouts that can help increase our spiritual energy and stamina. These practices have been both tested and written about by men and women who are spiritual trainers, and who have seen the results. In this chapter we will look at the exercises of engagement, that is, those practices that we move into to feed our soul and have a healthy heart. In the next chapter, we will look at the disciplines of disengagement, those practices of moving away from certain things to gain spiritual traction.

Some Disclaimers to Make

It is important to understand that the disciplines we are going to look at are simply tools. Not every tool will work for us in every situation. John Ortberg has said, "Spiritual growth is hand-crafted not mass-produced."[1] He goes on to say, "Spiritual disciplines are simply activities that make you more fully alive by the Spirit of Life."[2] John Wesley said of the spiritual disciplines, that they are "the means by which we receive grace."[3] These practices are not intended to show people how holy we are. They are meant to place our lives in an environment where we can hear God speak to us. What's most important is our motivation for practicing these spiritual behaviors. If the reason is anything other than desiring to know God and make Him known, we are disciplining ourselves for the wrong reasons. Let's take a look at some of the practices we can engage in to hear God's voice.

The Exercise of Worship

To have a healthy heart, the first discipline to consider practicing is worship. I appreciate Warren Wiersbe's definition of worship. "Worship is the believer's adoring response to all that God is, all that He has done, all that He says."[4] I would add one additional facet. Worship is responding to all that God has promised to do as well.

Worship is a response. It is all of a person, responding to a God who reveals Himself to that person. God reveals, and we respond in worship. Our individual response may vary. Some respond in worship with singing, others respond in praise or prayer, some raise their hands, others bow their head and heart and sometimes their knees before a holy and loving God.

Worship is important, because when leaders worship, two things happen. One is that the worshippers acknowledge that they are not the ones in control. They are bowing their will, heart, and emotions to the supreme leader, Jesus Christ.

A second and equally important phenomenon takes place when leaders worship. When we worship, we enter a place that the enemy of our soul knows nothing about. Satan does not know how to worship God, instead, he wants to be God. When the spiritual leader worships, he locks out the *"accuser of our brothers and sisters."* (Revelation 12:10) If you are feeling under attack these days, try worshipping.

We worship God in a variety of ways. We worship by praising Him, (Psalm 34:2,3) through music and singing, (Psalm 33:3, 66:2) by giving thanks, (Psalm 118:2) by telling of His wonderful acts, (Psalm 66:16, 107:2) by surrendering every part of our lives to God, (Romans 12:1) by being still (Psalm 46:10) and by serving God with a grateful heart. (Romans 12:1, Hebrews 13:15)

Finally, it is important to realize that true worship involves not just the emotions but also the mind (1 Corinthians 14:15) and the will. (Psalm 107:31,32) It is all of us responding to all that God is. Keep in mind that the Bible also describes worship as a war. There is an adversary that does not want to see us worship God. That's why it is even more important to spend time praising and thanking God to combat the enemy.

The result of worship is we become like the One we worship. The Apostle Paul tells us that we are transformed into the image of Christ. We become like Jesus. (2 Corinthians 3:18)

Living on the west coast, my family loves the sun. Whether it is my wife, three daughters or two sons, I can tell when they have been in the sun. They reflect it in their being. (Me, on the other hand, I fry in the sun and even break out into a rash.) The point is, when you spend time in the sun, people will notice. The same is true spiritually, when you spend time with the Son, you begin to reflect Him in your life. People will start to notice that you have been with Jesus.

The Exercise of Prayer

Have you ever asked yourself, "Why do I pray?" What is the purpose of praying? The Word of God says even before we pray that *"your Father knows exactly what you need even before you ask him!"* (Matthew 6:8) If this is true, then why pray? I believe there is a more important reason for praying than our asking or receiving anything.

While asking and receiving things in prayer is an important part of it, I think that God gave us the discipline of prayer to develop our relationship with Him. He wants us to know Him. We can't have a relationship with someone with whom we don't communicate. God wants us to learn to talk to Him, but He also desires that we spend time listening to Him in prayer. A simple tool that I have used for years in learning to listen in prayer is when I begin my prayer time; I simply ask the question, "God, what do you want me to pray about right now?" I then take the time to pause and listen for what God impresses upon me. This question prevents me from coming to God with a bad case of the " gimmes", and forces me to think about what God would want me to pray.

There are secondary reasons for praying that are important to consider as well. We pray because it aligns our will with God's. We pray to confess our sins to God. (1 John 1:9) Prayer is God's appointed way of receiving some things from Him. (Matthew 7:7) Prayer is God's way of helping us overcome worry and anxiety, and declare our dependence upon Him. (1 Peter 5:7) Finally, prayer is a way for us to refocus our heart and mind on heavenly things, not earthly impulses.

While there are many ways to pray, one of my favorite tools is using what has been called "The Lord's Prayer" as a guide.. In reality, this is the disciples' prayer, not the Lord's. Jesus could not have prayed all the words in this prayer. Instead, He gave His followers a guide to pray. This prayer is not meant to be recited word for word, but rather as a template to help us pray. Here is a way we can pray using the pattern that Jesus gave to us.

"Our Father" - **Personal–**The word that Jesus spoke here was Aramaic; it is the word "Abba." This word is the one of the most intimate words a child could utter. It means "papa" or "daddy." We give thanks to God, and that He is a personal God, who knows our situation.

"Who is in heaven, holy is Your Name" – **Praise–**God is above our circumstances. We spend time praising Him for who He is, what He has done and what He has promised to do.

"Your Kingdom come, Your will be done."- **Permission-** In this step we surrender our agenda to His, and we give God permission to do His work in us. This also has to do with our making Christ's kingdom and His values a priority in our lives.

"Give us this day our daily bread"- **Provision–**We ask God to provide our needs, whether they are financial, emotional, relational, spiritual or physical.

"Forgive us our debts as we forgive our debtors"- **Pardon–**We confess our sins to God and ask Him to help us forgive those who have hurt and offended us. While forgiving others

is a continual process of asking God for grace, it begins with a decision to ask God's help in letting it go.

"Lead us not into temptation, but deliver us from Evil"-**Protection**–Here we ask God to protect us against the things that will damage us, our family, our relationships and our integrity as a leader.

"Yours is the kingdom and the power and glory forever, Amen" **Power**–We ask God for His power in our life. We were not designed to live the Christian life on our own. We were created to cooperate with the Holy Spirit and rely on His power to live, overcome and bear fruit.

The Exercise of Bible Intake

It is critical that a spiritual leader is a person of the Book. We can dream dreams, think thoughts and think of innovative ideas, but we must sync them with God's Word and His will for them to have a spiritual impact. I am of the persuasion that there is not necessarily a specific verse to guide us in all of our decisions, but there are one or more guiding principles found in God's Word that can direct our decisions.

I also believe that God's Word is not any ordinary book. It is *"alive and powerful. It is sharper than the sharpest two-edged sword, cutting between soul and spirit, between joint and marrow. It exposes our innermost thoughts and desires."* (Hebrews 4:12)

God's Word speaks to the core of our being. Its goal is to transform the way we think, act and talk. It is not simply a historical document that is a collection of moral stories. It is God's Word to us. We believe the Bible to be trustworthy, because we believe that God is trustworthy, and He has preserved His Word to us so that we might know and follow Him.

What is most important is not getting into God's Word, but getting God's Word into us. I have met people who have read through the Bible many times, but they have not allowed the Bible to read them. They have been through the Bible, but the Bible has not been through them. I encourage people to read the Bible until God speaks to them. That may be a verse, a chapter, or if you are like me, sometimes it takes several chapters for me to slow down long enough to hear God.

There are multiple ways to get God's Word into our lives today. I recently used the hand illustration in one of our weekend messages. Our pinky finger represents *hearing* God's Word. The opportunity to hear God's Word has never been greater. With church apps and the internet, we can listen to God's Word being taught all day, if we so desire.

Our ring finger represents *reading* God's Word. At our church, we offer people a reading schedule at the New Year, and lovingly challenge people to read God's Word in its entirety. Those who are newer believers, we have a New Testament reading schedule. Again, there are a variety of reading plans available today that can fit your personal needs and schedule.

Our middle finger represents *studying* God's Word. The difference between reading and studying God's Word is slowing down and learning to ask questions of what we are reading. The inductive Bible Study method is centered around three main questions. First, *observation*, in other words, "What do I see?" What is going on in this passage? Who is writing? Why? To Whom? What kind of language is used here? What is the tone of the passage? What is the big idea? These are some of the questions we can ask during the observation stage of our study.

Second, is *interpretation*, in other words, "What does it mean?" In this step, we look for key words, repeated words, words we need to define, and basic grammar like conjunctions and the tense of a verb. We may consult resources like commentaries and concordances to understand the meaning of what we are studying.

Finally, is *application,* in other words, "What is this passage saying to me?" Application is where we ask God to show us how this applies to us personally. In order to avoid misinterpreting God's Word, it is important to work through the first two steps before jumping to this level. Is there a warning to heed? Is there a promise that we can claim? Is there a command we need to obey? Is there an example for us to follow?

Back to looking at our hand, our index finger represents *memorizing* God's Word. We will not always have our Bible with us, so committing God's Word to memory can help us both avoid tactical errors as well as moral failures. (Psalm 119:9,11) In Matthew 4, Jesus was tempted three times by the Devil, and each time He combatted the temptation by quoting the Old Testament that He had memorized.

Our thumb represents *meditating* on God's Word. This may seem a little mystic to some, but meditation is taking God's Word and recalling it regularly. The word meditate has been used to describe a cow chewing its cud. A cow grazes in the field and afterwards lies down in the field. A cow's stomach has several chambers, the heifer regurgitates what it has eaten and chews on it. After doing that, it sends it to the next chamber, and the process happens again. This is a rather crude picture of what meditation is. We graze on God's Word and then as we go through our day, we ruminate upon it regularly.

Rick Warren has said that if you know how to worry, then you already know how to meditate. When we worry, we meditate on our negative thoughts and fears. We visit the issue over and over with what might happen. It is believing the worst is going to happen.

When we meditate, we take a truth or promise found in God's Word and we marinate our minds in that verse or passage. As we do, we discover how to get God's perspective on the situation.

Finally, the last way to get a firm grip on God's Word is the *palm*. This represents *acting on* God's Word. Knowing God's Word is important, but knowing without doing is called hypocrisy. Paul made it clear that *"while knowledge makes us feel important, it is love that strengthens the church."* (1 Corinthians 8:1) If getting into God's Word does not prompt us to love God more passionately, others more compassionately and ourselves more correctly, we are missing the point of God's Word.

The Exercise of Generosity

One of the exercises that can help develop a healthy heart is the practice of generosity. Generosity can be defined as "the habit of giving without expecting anything in return. It can involve offering time, assets, or talents to aid someone in need."[5] (Wikipedia.com) I would also add that generosity often means sharing our financial resources and perhaps even our possessions. As we will see in this section, generosity is as much about an attitude of our hearts as it is an act of sacrifice.

Practicing generosity has a three-fold impact on our lives. This exercise is a flesh, faith and follow test. Let me explain. When we are willing to give to another without expectation of something in return, our flesh, the selfish side of us, always has a hard time. When we give our offering to the Lord, our flesh is often whispering in our ear, "That's too much!" or "You can't afford to do that!" Practicing generosity keeps our flesh in check. When we are generous, we are demonstrating that our flesh is not our master, but our servant. Generosity forces us to deny ourselves and think of others as more important.

This exercise of generosity also is a faith test. Each time we give something away whether it is our time, talents or treasure, we believe by faith that God will provide and take care of us. We are showing that God is the ultimate owner of our resources and that if He leads us to be generous to others, we will trust that He will meet our needs in return. It is an ownership issue.

Finally, exercising generosity is a follow test. If we desire to be like Jesus, we must be willing to serve and sacrifice. As one pastor said, "you can give without loving, but you can't love without giving." If we say we love God and others, we must show it by laying down our life for our friends.

Several years ago, I heard a message by Warren Wiersbe on the type of giving that pleases God. I have never forgotten that message. Dr. Wiersbe drew these principles from Paul's second letter to the Corinthians in chapters eight and nine. Let me briefly share them with you.

First, the type of generosity that pleases God is when we give in spite of our circumstances. Paul wrote about the churches in Macedonia, *"They are tested by many troubles, and they are very poor. But they are also filled with abundant joy, which has overflowed in rich generosity."* (2 Corinthians 8:2) Notice the adjectives that Paul uses here. Would you circle the words many, very, abundant and rich? Paul said that in spite of their suffering and poverty, they exercised generosity.

Our circumstances will never promote generosity. We will always be able to find a reason not to give. Generosity is an attitude of our heart, but it is also an act of our will. There may be times when the feelings and emotions of generosity may not be there.

Secondly, generosity that comes from a pure heart is done out of a heart of love. Paul writes these words, *"Since you excel in so many ways-in your faith, your gifted speakers, your knowledge, your enthusiasm, and your love for us- I want you to excel also in this gracious act of giving."* (2

Corinthians 8:7) Giving that honors God comes from a heart of love for God and His people.

Thirdly, generosity that pleases God is that which is done willingly and worshipfully. We are not to give *"reluctantly or in response to pressure."* (2 Corinthians 9:7) We give because God is a generous God, and we can never out-give Him. We give out a heart of worship, not for recognition or accolades, but because we love Jesus and want to be like Him.

Fourthly, God-pleasing giving is exercised without the expectation of something in return. We don't give to get something. That is not the Jesus way. Over the years, I have been invited to listen to a presentation by various multi-level marketing representatives. They have tried to persuade me that the organization is Christian and how it is founded on Christian principles. The dialogue usually stalls out when I ask them if they can show me in the Bible where it says we are to serve others so that we will get something in return from them. I have asked this question on frequent occasions, "Where does it say that we are to help others so that by doing so, we benefit ourselves?" Don't we serve and give to others because it's the Jesus thing to do? Did Jesus serve and sacrifice to benefit Himself? No! Jesus gave out of a heart of pure love, because He wanted what was best for us, because He wanted a relationship with us personally, and intimately, because He would rather die than live without us.

God does not promise if we give, we will always receive material things in return. Paul states, *"Now he who supplies seed to the sower and bread for food will also supply and increase your store of seed and will enlarge the harvest of your righteousness. You will be enriched in every way so that you can be generous on every occasion."* (2 Corinthians 9:10-11) Notice this verse says, God will increase our spiritual harvest and enrich us in every way, not just in a material return.

We are never more like God than when we give from a heart of love. The one thing the church has done throughout the centuries, whether it is the founding of hospitals for the sick, rescue missions for the homeless, shelters for the downtrodden or care ministries for the hurting, has been to show Jesus' love by not just telling, but also by showing God's love through generosity.

The Exercise of Gratitude

A practice that is closely related to generosity is the attitude of gratitude. Recently, I had a couple come into my office because they were experiencing some marital struggles. During our time together they both shared with me that after a couple of decades of marriage, the fun and closeness of marriage had worn thin. They were missing each other emotionally and relationally.

While they were talking, I thought about the church at Ephesus, and how they had lost their first love. John wrote that they were to repent, which means change their thinking, and do the things they did at first. (Revelation 2:4-5)

I challenged this couple that before the next time we met, they make a list of the top ten things that they were attracted to in each other, and none of them could be physically related. Honestly, I wasn't sure they would follow through, but when we met again they both came in with their list. I asked them to read it to each other. When they finished reading, they were both in tears. I encouraged them to put that list in a place where they would see it often. I encouraged them to read over that list for the next week. What had happened was they had forgotten their first love. Exercising gratitude is God's way of helping us remember our first love. As we practice being grateful, our hearts become free from the "when and then" syndrome, and we are able to be content in the here and now.

A key to a healthy relationship with Christ is to recognize and remember all the things He has done for us. I encourage you to make a gratitude list for the next seven days. List at least ten things you are thankful for each day and see if it changes your perspective on living and leading. As I have practiced this discipline I have found myself enjoying my children more, and I have found that my relationships were enhanced.

Just like worship, when we exercise gratitude, we are entering a place of which Satan knows nothing. Our enemy is full of greed, not gratitude. He wanted the glory that rightfully belonged to God, and wants us to do the same. Gratitude promotes humility and contentment, neither of which the Devil desires, either for himself, or for us as spiritual leaders.

The Exercise of Service

If you are like me, you are good at serving others. A large part of our job as spiritual leaders is serving those who follow. To do so with the right heart and the right motives is always a challenge.

I love the way Paul lays out Romans 12. He begins with the language of worship. He says that we are to offer our lives in surrender to God as a living sacrifice. We give ourselves to Him. We spend time worshipping Him.

Paul then moves to the importance of renewing our mind in verse two. He says we need to be separate from this world's system by renewing our minds. God is more concerned about changing our thinking than He is about changing our circumstances. We do this by practicing any or all of the above mentioned exercises.

He then moves to challenging his readers to have an accurate view of themselves. I like defining humility as "seeing yourself as God sees you, nothing more, nothing less.[6]" Knowing who we are in Christ and how our identity is in Him, and not in what we do, sets the stage for service.

Paul, after saying all of this, then moves into service. Serving others must come from a heart of worship, a renewed mind, a correct understanding of who we are in Christ. Once we understand these things we can then properly serve others.

I once used a couple of Styrofoam cups to illustrate this point. I told the staff we can serve God in two ways, and I put water in both cups. I punctured a hole in the bottom of one cup and said, that we can drain our life into the life of someone else. If we take this approach, we will eventually burn out. A second way to serve is like this I took water and poured it into the cup until it overflowed into the other cup. God wants us to serve Him out of the overflow of what He has done for us and who we are in Christ. If we don't understand this, we will easily serve people with the wrong motives. Soon our hearts will grow cold and we will simply go through the motions. When that happens it won't be long before the cup is drained completely, and there is nothing more to give.

The Exercise of Journaling

There have been many people throughout the centuries who have used journaling as a way to engage with God. The popular devotionals such as "My Utmost for His Highest," and "Jesus Calling," were originally journal entries by the writers that were later turned into devotionals.

Writing out our thoughts can help us clarify our thinking, off-load stress, promote an intense time of prayer as well as help us sort through the complexities of life. King David, (Many of the Psalms) King Solomon (the book of Ecclesiastes), the Apostle Paul (2 Corinthians) as well as John (Revelation), all made journal entries that are now viewed at as chapters or entire books of the Bible.

The exercise of journaling has many different forms. It can contain lists, prayers, thoughts, or even goals. Many bloggers use their journal as a way of collecting topics to write their blogs. There are some great software programs such as "Day One" or "Evernote" that can help you journal electronically.

Journaling may not be for everyone. As I heard one speaker say, "I don't recall reading anywhere the Jesus journaled." You don't have to keep a journal to be like Jesus but it can help in your pursuit to take one step closer to Him.

The Exercise of Curiosity

I believe one of the reasons that people become complacent in their life, their job; their marriage is because they don't stay curious. I love to watch my fifteen-month old twin grandsons. Their level of curiosity is at an all time high. They continue to amaze me at what they get into in their desire to explore their world.

Recently, my daughter relayed a story in which she stepped out of her condominium to put one of the boys in the stroller, and the other one locked her out. He proceeded to get up on their couch and grab the remote and watch TV. (They learn young, don't they?) After a call to the Fire Department, they were able to get in through the sliding glass door and rescue her toddler.

I pray for a spirit of curiosity like my grandsons. May we continue to engage in wonder, creativity and creation in order to see more clearly the hand of our Creator. May we practice this in our marriages with our spouse and our children. Staying curious can keep our hearts growing and going.

These are some of the exercises we need to engage in to keep our heart hot. I want to challenge you before we move to the next chapter and look at the disciplines of detachment, that you choose one of these exercises and make a commitment to practice it this week.

Talk it Over:

1. Which of the above disciplines resonates the most with you?

2. Which one would you consider a growth area?

3. What will you do this week to practice one or more of these exercises of engagement?

Digging Deeper:

Foster, Richard. *The Celebration of Discipline: The Path to Spiritual Growth*. New York: HarperCollins Publishers, 1978.

Whitney, Donald. *Spiritual Disciplines for the Christian Life*. Colorado Springs: NavPress, 2014.

Chapter 21

Heart Healthy Habits- Part 2: The Disciplines of Detachment

"The spiritual disciplines are a means to an end, not an end in themselves. They are designed to help us see God more clearly so that we can glorify Him more personally."
Richard Foster

My son has had a couple of opportunities to workout with some NFL players. It has always amazed me how much time these athletes put in to both getting and staying fit. It's not unusual for them to go from lifting weights one hour, to playing a full court basketball game the next. Many of these players spend an entire day at the gym during the off-season. I have always marveled at the discipline of a devoted athlete. Part of their training is learning to disengage from certain things in order to prepare themselves for the upcoming season.

In the last chapter we looked at some exercises of engagement, those practices that put us in a place for God to reveal Himself to us. In this chapter we want to see several of the disciplines of disengagement. When we practice these habits, we intentionally disengage ourselves from certain things so that we can more clearly hear God speak to us. Let's take a look.

The Discipline of Fasting

The discipline of fasting throughout the centuries has been misunderstood and misapplied. Even in Jesus' day, the Pharisees abused this discipline as a way to demonstrate their superior morality. It became a way to bring attention to themselves, both by their appearance as well as their practice.

There are several definitions for fasting that have been given. "Fasting is the abstaining from food for spiritual purposes,"[1] "In fasting, we give up something for the sake of something better." Another definition of fasting is, "abstinence from food/drink as an element of private or public religious devotion."[2] One of my favorite books on the subject of fasting is John Piper's book, *"A Hunger for God."* The premise of the book is that we fast because we are desperately hungry for God to bring a breakthrough in our lives and our world. We are so hungry for God to reveal His glory to us that we are willing to do without food or other material things so that we can hear from God. Piper writes, "Ultimately, we fast simply because we want God more than we want anything this world has to offer." [3] He further states that, "Christian fasting, at its root, is the hunger, homesickness for God." [4] "The more deeply you walk with Christ, the hungrier you get *for* Christ . . . the more homesick you get for heaven . . . the more you want 'all the fullness of God'...the more you want to be done with sin...the more you want the Bridegroom to come again . . . the more you want the Church revived and purified with the beauty of Jesus."[5]

While fasting from food is the most common type of fasting, there may be other kinds of fasts as well. Detaching from things like television, social media, phones, computers, caffeine or other things a person may feel has a hold on their lives are also other forms of fasting. Fasting may involve giving up a meal, going a day without food, and for some, even a forty-day fast has been done, drinking only liquids.

Personally, on a much smaller scale, I decided a while back to give up drinking all soda. After decades of feeding my addiction to carbonation, I have decided to do without. I can honestly say I don't miss it, I feel better about myself, and I realize that if God can change this one small area of my life, He's not done with me in other areas of my being.

Some people may ask the reasons for fasting. The Bible is full of reasons to spend time in prayer and fasting. People fasted in the Old Testament to enhance their relationship with God, (Zechariah 7:5) to break the bonds of wickedness and heaviness, (Isaiah 58:7) to humble themselves before the Lord and confess their sin. (Daniel 9:2-7) I think the most important reason for fasting is so that we can hear from God. We fast to sharpen our listening to God and to seek Him for direction. (Acts 13:2) Even as we experience the pain of hunger, we can use those hunger pangs as a way to depend on God to fill us with His grace. Richard Foster says, "more than any other discipline, fasting reveals the things that control us." [6]

The Discipline of Solitude

The discipline of solitude can be defined as detaching from interacting with people for the purpose of being alone with God to hear from Him, speak to Him, reflect on our life and the lives of others, and simply be with Him.

One of my all-time favorite verses when working with spiritual leaders is Acts 4:13. When Peter and John were arrested for sharing their faith openly and healing a man publicly, those who accused them came this realization: *"The members of the Council were amazed when they saw the boldness of Peter and John, for they could see that they were ordinary men with no special training in the Scriptures. They also recognized them as men who had been with Jesus.*" The one distinguishing feature of Peter and John is that they had been with Jesus. Solitude is simply "being with Jesus."

Throughout the Bible we are instructed to spend time in stillness before the Lord. The most familiar verse is Psalm 46:10, *"Be still, and know that I am God."* David wrote elsewhere, *"I wait quietly before God, for my victory comes from him."* (Psalm 62:1) and *"But as for me, how good it is to be near God! I have made the Sovereign LORD my shelter, and I will tell everyone about the wonderful things you do."* (Psalm 73:28)

Henri Nouwen writes, "It is better to have a daily practice of ten minutes of solitude than to have a whole hour once in a while. Simplicity and regularity are the best guides in finding our way. They allow us to make the discipline of solitude as much a part of our daily lives as eating and sleeping. When that happens, our noisy worries will slowly lose their power over us, and the renewing activity of God's Spirit will slowly make its presence known." [7]

From the New Testament we know that on multiple occasions, Jesus spent time alone with the Father. As the demands on His time and energy increased, He spent extended time alone in solitude, sometimes all night seeking the Father's heart. (Matthew 14:23, Mark 1:35)

Jesus' invitation to us is found in Matthew 11:28-30. I love how Eugene Peterson in the Message translates this offer, *"Are you tired? Worn out? Burned out on religion? Come to me. Get away with me and you'll recover your life. I'll show you how to take a real rest. Walk with me and work with me-watch how I do it. Learn the unforced rhythms of grace. I won't lay anything heavy or ill-fitting on you. Keep company with me and you'll learn to live freely and lightly."*

So let me ask you, friend, do people see that you have been with Jesus? Do they recognize it in your words, your actions, and your countenance? Is your soul telling you it's time to disengage and get alone with the Father? I want to encourage you right now to stop reading this book and put a time on your calendar when you will detach into solitude.

The Discipline of Sabbath

The discipline of Sabbath can be described as detaching from our normal work to rest in God's person and provision. It may involve praying, playing or resting. Taking a Sabbath rest allows us to renew physically, spiritually and emotionally.

Throughout the Bible, God established a one in seven rhythm to life. Upon creation of the world, it says that God rested. (Genesis 2:2) Why did God rest? Was it that He was tired from a long week of creating things? Was He worried knowing what was ahead in chapter three, that all of His creation would be severely thrashed by sin? No, God rested to model for us what is most important in life. Mark Buchannan in his superb book called *The Rest of God* says, "Sabbath is both a day an attitude to nurture such stillness. It is both time on a calendar and a disposition of the heart."[8] Whenever we detach into a Sabbath rest, we are surrendering control and acknowledging that we are not God. Even the President of the United States has to surrender control every night when he turns the lights out and gets some rest.

When God gave His commandments to His people, He instructed them, *"You have six days each week for your ordinary work, but the seventh day is a Sabbath day of rest dedicated to the LORD your God. On that day no one in your household may do any work."* (Exodus 20:9,10) Why would God require this of His people? One reason was that to do no work on the Sabbath was an exercise in faith. These people had no refrigeration like we have today, and if they ceased to work and produce, they would have to trust God that He would preserve and protect the work of the previous six days.

They said, "God, I trust You enough that if I honor You on this day, You will provide my needs."

For many reading these pages, Sunday is not a day of rest. It is the time of the week you are most engaged with people and responsibilities. Many of you will need to designate another day to renew, refresh and re-create.

When it comes to the New Testament, Jesus did not do away with the Sabbath, but put a new twist on its purpose. The religious leaders of the day made the Sabbath a measurement of spirituality. Not only did they make this day a strict adherence, they began to define kinds of work that was allowed based on their own man-made conclusions. Over time, they perverted the purpose of the Sabbath into a checklist of do's and don'ts. Jesus stepped into this pseudo-spiritual arena and made this radical declaration, *"The Sabbath was made to meet the needs of people, and not people to meet the requirements of the Sabbath."* (Mark 2:27)

The Sabbath is a tool to be used to center our minds, hearts and bodies on the Lord of the Sabbath, Jesus Christ. I love what Buchannan writes, "Sabbath imparts the rest of God- actual physical, mental, spiritual rest, but also the rest of God-the things of God's nature and presence we miss in our busyness."[9] Observing the Sabbath is a really a symbol of our freedom. He further writes, "To refuse the Sabbath is in effect to spurn the gift of freedom. It is to resume willingly what we once cried out for God to deliver us from. It is choosing what we once shunned. Slaves don't rest. Slaves can't rest. Slaves by definition, have no freedom to rest. Rest, it turns out, is a condition of liberty. God calls us to live in the freedom that He won for us with His own outstretched arm. Sabbath is a refusal to go back to Egypt."[10]

The Discipline of Simplicity

The discipline of simplicity can be defined as detaching from things to live a simple, focused life. It is choosing to refuse to put our value and identity in what we own or how much we make.

While this discipline may seem to only relate to material possessions, it can also relate to our schedules, our finances, our commitments and many other areas of our life. In an interview with *Leadership Journal*, Pastor Bill Hybels says that we need to practice the discipline of "strategic neglect." He mentions that it is tempting to try and understand multiple complex issues in a single day. But we have to say, "I will strategically neglect that issue so that I can really wrap my head, my heart, and my energy around what God has assigned to me."[11]

The choices you will be asked to make as a leader are not always between good and bad, they may often be between good and best. If you are a reliable, responsible and effective leader you will be in high demand. People will want your involvement in their circles. You will have to decide between what's good and what's best for you, your ministry or your family.

"To sustain high levels of passion for decades, you have to have certain disciplines, routines, and practices."[12] The exercises of engagement and the disciplines of detachment can help sustain the joy, passion, and endurance you need to thrive even in the most difficult seasons of leadership.

Recently, my cell phone has not been keeping a charge. It quickly fades if not hooked up to the charger. A few days ago, I went to use my phone, and discovered that I hadn't hooked it up to the charger. The charger was lying right next to my phone, but I failed to plug it in. The result was no connection and no power.

These disciplines are designed to help you recharge your spiritual batteries so that you can connect with God and those around you. They are simply a way you can plug in to God's life and power. If one of them doesn't work for you, try another. Find a method and system that works for you. It may take a few attempts in a discipline before you find one that fits but don't stop attempting to find ways to keep the connection open and alive.

Talk it Over:

1. What is the purpose of the spiritual disciplines?

2. Which of the mentioned spiritual disciplines in this chapter, have you tried in the past? What were the results?

3. Which of the mentioned spiritual disciplines in this chapter are you challenged by God to practice this week?

Digging Deeper:

Buchanan, Mark. *The Rest of God*. Nashville: Thomas Nelson, 2006.

Hybels, Bill. *Simplify: Ten Practices to Unclutter Your Soul*. Carol Stream: Tyndale, 2014.

Ortberg, John. *The Life You Always Wanted: Spiritual Disciplines for Ordinary People*. Grand Rapids: Zondervan, 2002.

Conclusion

"Run the Court and Pass the Ball"

*"It's better to look ahead and prepare
than to look back and regret."*
Tom Mullins

O nce upon a time when I played basketball, our coach
had us do a drill in practice called the "weave." It consisted of three players standing on the end line, one in the middle and one on each side. On the coach's whistle the players took off, the player in the middle having the ball. The idea was the ball could not be dribbled. It had to be passed all the way down the court. Each time the passer let go of the ball he would move to one of the other player's positions. When the trio approached the opposite end, the player in the middle would stop at the top of the key and bounce pass it to one of the other players who would go up for a layup. The three players would then repeat the drill all the way back to where they started.

The purpose of this exercise was intended to provide multiple outcomes. It was designed to teach the players passing skills, fast break skills, as well as teamwork. Most importantly, it was designed to teach players how to run the court and pass the ball. Our coach knew that the best teams learn how to share the ball and look for the open player.

What will you do with what you have read?

As leaders, we are faced with a similar drill. In this book I have attempted to give you a full court look at what a leader looks and acts like. Now the time has come to ask the question, "What will you do with what you have read?" How is knowing the information contained in this book going to change the way you lead?

On a personal level, how are you going to implement the things we have looked at and discussed? What will you do to take your leadership to a new level? How can you raise your leadership leverage? If all you do is read these pages and make no plan to follow through on practicing these concepts, this book will be put back on a shelf along with the rest of your books, and I will have spent a good portion of my life writing about lofty ideas, but little transformation will take place.

I want to encourage you to pause for a moment and think back on one or two areas in which you would like to grow personally and see God develop in your life. Ask Him to help you to discern which areas you want to start focusing on first. Invite God into the process of self-discovery. In each of the chapters, I have included a few resources for further exploration. I encourage you to pick up any of those or others that may help you with your leadership deficiencies. The time has come to run the court and be a full court leader.

Secondly, it's important to pass the ball. This material is not designed for you to keep to yourself. I hope you will identify others that you may invite to journey with you through this material. You can use it one-on-one, in a mentoring group or even with a small group of emerging leaders. I want to encourage you to think and pray about someone that you can take through *Leadership for L.I.F.E.*

I have chosen to write this book on a practical rather than a technical level so that people who are in the trenches of leadership can easily adapt this material to their leadership context. My desire is that this resource would be helpful to many people struggling to understand what it means to be a leader, particularly a spiritual leader.

Tom Mullins in his book, *Passing the Leadership Baton*, says that, "the baton of leadership is not yours to keep."[1] The goal of leadership is to empower and equip others. Someone has said if you make it a goal to work yourself out of a job, you will always have a job. With that in mind, let me offer a few closing suggestions.

- **Begin praying about inviting someone to go through this material with you**

As we have already said, people respond best to a personal invitation. Take a few moments to get a blank index card out and write the names of one or more people you can ask to join you on this journey. There are people in your circles of leadership that would be honored to have someone come alongside of them and help them discover how to be the leader God intended.

- **Continue working on improving your leadership**

The fact that you read this book indicates your desire to improve. I want to encourage you, don't stop. The moment you stop learning as a leader, is the moment you stop growing, the moment you stop growing is the moment you stop leading. This material is called "Leadership for L.I.F.E." because I firmly believe that leadership is a life-long journey.

Rick Warren tells the story about being in a meeting with W.A. Criswell, who at the time was in his eighties and pastoring one of the largest churches in America. Rick was impressed that Dr. Criswell sat in the meeting with a pen and notepad in hand taking notes as he continued to learn about leadership.

I thought to myself, I want to be that kind of person. I want to be found during my last days here on Earth, as someone who is learning how to do this thing called leadership better. I hope someday that someone will find me when I take my last breath with a pen and notepad in hand learning to be more like Jesus.

- **The journey of leadership is a journey toward Jesus**

The best leader we can learn from is Jesus Christ. He came to show us how effective leadership happens. The result is that his followers changed the world with their leadership. If this book has helped you take one step closer to Jesus then it has all been worth it.

So my final challenge to you is to run the court and pass the ball. See what God has in store for you as you do. I would love to hear the story of how God has used this material in your life and leadership. You can contact me at <u>Lead4Him1@ aol.com</u>.

Going Deeper:

Maxwell, John C. *Developing the Leaders Around You: How to Help Others Reach Their Full Potential.* (Nashville: Thomas Nelson, 2003).

Mullins, Tom. *Passing the Leadership Baton.* (Nashville: Thomas Nelson, 2015).

Stanley, Andy. *Next Generation Leader: 5 Essentials for Those who Shape the Future.* (Colorado Springs: Multnomah Books, 2003).

Notes

Chapter 1- Is there a Leader in the House?

1. Dictionary.com. Accessed February, 2016. http:// www.dictionary.com/.
2. John C. Maxwell, *Developing the Leader Within You* (Nashville: Thomas Nelson, 1993), 1.
3. J. Oswald Sander, *Spiritual Leadership* (Chicago: Moody Press, 2007), 22.
4. Henry Blackaby, *Spiritual Leadership: Moving People on to God's Agenda* (Nashville: Broadman & Holman Publishers, 2001), 36.
5. Ibid., 32.
6. Maxwell, *Developing the Leader Within You, 41.*

Chapter 2- The Leadership Leverage

1. James M. Kouzes and Barry Z. Posner, *Credibility: How Leaders Gain and Lose it, Why People Demand It* (San Francisco: Jossey-Bass, 2011), 8.
2. Dictionary.com. Accessed March 15, 2016. http:// www.dictionary.com/.
3. Most secondary sources attribute this quote to John C. Maxwell. Primary source not located.

4. "How Pure Must a Leader be? An interview with Chuck Swindoll. *Building Church Leaders,* Christianity Today International, Wheaton, IL,2000.

5. John C. Maxwell, *Developing the Leader Within You: Workbook* (Nashville: Thomas Nelson, 2001), 63.

6. John C. Maxwell, *3 Things Successful People Do: The Road Map That Will Change Your Life* (Nashville: Thomas Nelson, 2016), 93.

7. Bronnie Ware, "Top 5 Regrets of the Dying" *The Huffington Post,* January 21, 2012, www.huffpost.com/goodnews.

Chapter 3- Building Your Trust Fund

1. Dictionary.com. Accessed March 15, 2016. http://www.dictionary.com/.

2. Stephen M.R. Covey and Greg Link, *Smart Trust: The Defining Skill that Transforms Managers into Leaders* (New York: Free Press, 2012), 79.

3. "Trust But Verify." Wikipedia. Accessed March 12, 2016. http://www.wikipedia.com/.

4. John C. Maxwell, *Winning With People: Discover the Principles That Work for You Every Time* (Nashville: Thomas Nelson, 2004), 91.

5. Stephen M.R. Covey, *The Speed of Trust: The One Thing that Changes Everything,* (New York: Free Press, 2006), xxv.

6. Covey, *The Speed of Trust,* condensed from the list given on pp. 22-24.

Chapter 4- Leading with a Towel

1. *Undercover Boss,* "1-800-Flowers," CBS, April 11, 2010.

Chapter 5- Impossible or Him Possible?

1. Max Lucado, *Inspirational Reader: Hope and Encouragement for Your Everyday* (Nashville: Thomas Nelson, 2011), 153.
2. Ben Lowe and Ajith Fernando, *Doing Good Without Giving Up: Sustaining Social Action in a World that's Hard to Change* (Downers Grove: InterVarsity Press, 2014), 92.
3. David J. Bagget, Gary R. Habermas, Jerry L. Walls, Thomas V. Morris, *C.S. Lewis as Philosopher: Truth, Goodness and Beauty* (Downers Grove: InterVarsity Press, 2008), 204.

Chapter 7- Growth Spurts

1. Amy Charmichael, *Edges of His Ways: Selections for Daily Readings* (Fort Washington: CLC Publications, 1955), 175-176.
2. Chip Ingram and Becca Johnson, *Overcoming Emotions that Destroy! Practical Help for those Angry Feelings that Ruin Relationships* (Grand Rapids: Baker Books, 2009), 49-66.

Chapter 8- Listen Like a Leader

1. Michael P. Nichols, *The Lost Art of Listening* (New York: Guilford Publications Inc., 1995), 22.
2. Ibid., 88.
3. Ibid., (paraphrased from pp. 68-74).
4. Ibid., , 72.

Chapter 9- I Can See Clearly Now: Developing a Compelling Vision

1. George Barna, *The Power of Vision: Discover and Apply God's Plan for Your Life and Ministry* (Ventura: Regal Books, 2009), 23.
2. Aubrey Malphurs, *Planting Churches for the 21st Century: A Comprehensive Guide for New Churches and Those Desiring Renewal* (Grand Rapids: Baker Books, 2004), 100.
3. Andy Stanley, *Visioneering: God's Blueprint for Developing and Maintaining Personal Vision* (Colorado Springs: Multnomah Books, 1999), 18.
4. Source Unknown.

Chapter 10- Go S.T.A.R.T. Something

1. David R. Mains, *Healing the Dysfunctional Church Family.* (Shippensburg: Destiny Image, 1992) 114.
2. Michael Hyatt, "The Five Levels of Delegation," *Your Virtual Mentor* (blog), October 14, 2010, http://www.michaelhyatt.com.
3. John C. Maxwell and Leslie Parrot. *25 Ways to Win with People: How to Make Others Feel Like a Million Bucks* (Nashville: Thomas Nelson, 2005), 111.
4. John Borek, Danny Lovett and Elmer Towns, *The Good Book on Leadership: Case Studies from the Bible* (Nashville: Broadman & Holman Publishers, 2005), 55.
5. Source Unknown.
6. Aubrey Malphurs, *Look Before You Lead: How to discern and Shape Your Church Culture* (Grand Rapids: Baker Books, 2013) 95-98.
7. Max De Pree. *Leadership is an Art.* (New York: Random House, 2004), 28.

8. Craig Groeschel, *Catalyst One Day, Livermore, CA,* March 2015.

Chapter 12- When Leadership Comes with a Microphone

1. Stephen E. Olford and David L. Olford, *Anointed Expository Preaching* (Nashville: Broadman & Holman Publishers, 1998), 233.
2. Henry Blackaby, *Spiritual Leadership: Moving People on to God's Agenda* (Nashville: Broadman & Holman Publishers, 2001), 192-193.
3. J. Scott Duvall and J. Daniel Hays, *Grasping God's Word* (Grand Rapids: Zondervan, 2012) 149.
4. David Helm, *Expository Preaching: How We Speak God's Word* (Wheaton: Crossway, 2014) 16.

Chapter 13- Time Keeps on Slipping

1. Charles R. Swindoll, *Living on the Ragged Edge* (Nashville: Thomas Nelson, 2004), 53-54.
2. Stephen R. Covey, *The Seven Habits of Highly Effective People: Powerful Lessons in Personal Change* (New York: Simon & Schuster, 2004), 60.
3. **Dictionary.com, cited July 1st, 2016.**

Chapter 14- Giving Spiritual Counsel Without Being the Counselor

1. Heather Zempel, *Community is Messy* (Downers Grove: InterVarsity Press, 2012), 32-33.
2. Joe McKeever, *21 Things Not to Say to a Hurting Friend, www.churchleaders.com* November 13, 2014.

Chapter 15- Navigating Through Conflict

1. Emerson Eggerich, *Cracking the Communication Code: The Secrets to Speaking Your Mate's Language* (Nashville: Thomas Nelson, 2007), 32.
2. Ken Sande, *Resolving Everyday Conflict* (Grand Rapids: Baker Books, 2011), 11.
3. Nancy Leigh Demoss, *"I Don't Want to Heart it"* Revive our Hearts Radio, February 10, 2011.

Chapter 16- How to Deal with Criticism

1. Donald T. Phillips, *Lincoln on Leadership: Strategies for Tough Times* (New York: Warner Books, 1992), 72.
2. Ibid., 70.

Chapter 17- Discovering Your Own S.T.O.R.Y.

1. Dr. Stephen Graves, *The Hero Leader: Why Effective Leaders Combine Strengths and Weaknesses.* (Fayetteville: KJK Inc. Publishers, 2014), 24.
2. Ibid., 9.

Chapter 18- The Shadows of Leadership

1. Warren W. Wiersbe, *The Bible Exposition Commentary* (Wheaton: Victor Books, 1989), 342.
2. Gordon MacDonald, *Ordering Your Private World* (Nashville: Thomas Nelson, 2003), 32-39.
3. Gary McIntosh and Samuel D. Rima Jr., *The Dark Side of Leadership* (Grand Rapids: Baker Books, 1997), 119.

Chapter 19- The Heart of a Leader

1. Andy Stanley, *How to Be Rich: It's Not What You Have, It's What You do with What You Have,* (Grand Rapids: Zondervan, 2013), 33.
2. Sandra Wilson, *Hurt People, Hurt People* (Grand Rapids: Discovery House Publishers, 2001), 209.

Chapter 20- Heart Healthy Habits Part 1: Exercises of Engagement

1. John Ortberg and John Rubin, *The Me I Want to Be, Teen Edition: Becoming God's Best Version of You."* (Grand Rapids,: Zondervan, 2010), 41.
2. Ibid., 42.
3. " Millay, Chris. "Temptations." Pastorphers Weblog. February 14, 2016. http://pastorpher.wordpress.com/.
4. Warren W. Wiersbe, *Prayers, Praise and Promises: A Daily Walk Through the Psalms* (Grand Rapids: Baker Books, 2011), 261.
5. "Generosity." Wikipedia. Accessed April 04, 2016. http://www.wikipedia.com/.
6. Carolyn Larson and Rick Incorocci, *What Does the Bible say About That?* (Wheaton: Crossway Books, 2009.

Chapter 21- Heart Healthy Habits, Part 2: Disciplines of Detachment

1. Richard Foster, *The Celebration of Discipline* (San Francisco: Harper and Row, 1978), 40.
2. "Fasting." Bible Study Tools. Accessed March 01, 2016. http://www.biblestudytools.com/.
3. John Piper, *A Hunger for God* (Wheaton: Crossway Books, 1997), 11.

4. Ibid.,17.
5. Ibid.,25.
6. Foster, *The Celebration of Discipline*, 22.
7. Henri Nouwen, *An Introduction to Solitude*, excerpted from Leadership Journal, Fall 1981.
8. Mark Buchanan, *The Rest of God* (Nashville, TN: Thomas Nelson, 2006), 3.
9. Ibid.,3.
10. Ibid.,90.
11. *The Secret of Strategic Neglect,* Bill Hybels (an interview with Leadership Journal, Winter 2015)
12. Ibid

Conclusion- Run the Court and Pass the Ball

1. Tom Mullins, *Passing the Leadership Baton.* (Nashville: Thomas Nelson, 2015), 22.

CPSIA information can be obtained
at www.ICGtesting.com
Printed in the USA
FSOW04n1636021116
26891FS